Story
CONTINUES...

CHOOSING CRAZY FAITH OVER CRIPPLING FEAR

BETHANY BRYAN

Published by HigherLife Development Services Inc.
  PO Box 623307
  Oviedo, Florida 32762
  www.ahigherlife.com

ISBN: 978-1-954533-28-8 (Paperback)
ISBN: 978-1-954533-29-5 (ebook)
Library of Congress Control Number: 1-10418615041

10 9 8 7 6 5 4 3 2 1

SCENES

INTRODUCTION

"God never wastes a hurt." I am a firm believer in that saying, and through reading this book, I hope you will become one too. We all go through times of trial to bring growth, and that growth isn't just for us, but to share with those around us. That is what I am hoping to accomplish with this book.

Each battle I have faced, no matter how personal, has taught me something. My story may be odd to those who have never experienced the battle between reality and faith. There are moments where faith feels more real than reality itself, and you enjoy the difference so much that reality becomes a disappointment. After that opening, you are probably thinking, "I should have left this quack on the shelf." But now you're out a few bucks so you might as well read through the first chapter. I promise you will get something out of this book!

"A brilliant storyteller"—that's what I have been told I am. With my flair for the arts, I love being both behind and in front of the camera. But where I find I'm most gifted at is in the creative process of writing. I found it difficult to tell you my story without the dramatic flair I tend to write with, but I also tell stories verbally very differently from how I write them, with comedic timing and occasional rabbit trails. You will notice both ways throughout this book. As much as I tried to be consistent, this is who I am.

The first chapter will be for you to get to know me. I am a firm believer in references. I want you to not just hear about me through my own words, but through those who have watched me fight, fall, fail, and triumph. Through their perspectives, you can get an idea of who I am as a person before you get into how I became the way I am. I have not bribed them to give a good report; in fact, these people have walked beside me through my most intimate and vulnerable moments. I have given them total liberty to spill any and all beans they wish, and to tell you the truth on how they have dealt with my journey in their own way. Not everyone comes from the same faith background, but I think it's important to hear from all perspectives. After the first chapter, you will then read my story through my eyes, which involves some crazy but true events, fun facts, and a forever-switching timeline. But that's just how I felt I needed to tell it.

Maybe you're reading this book for encouragement because you have been sick and need a miracle. Or maybe you just liked the photo on the cover of my cute face. Whatever the reason, you are supposed to read this book. Perhaps some words in this book will end up being a lifeline in a time of confusion or struggle. Then my story will help your story, which is good. This is how I went from patient to patience. You're confused already, huh? Just read it.

Acknowledgments

First and foremost, I want to acknowledge GOD, the Father, Son, and Holy Spirit. You are the beat of my heart.

To my amazing family, Daddy Warren, Mommy Melissa, Sista' Tearsa-Joy, and Bubba Chris, you guys are the sugar to my tea. (That's really important because unsweet tea is from the pits of hell, so sugar is like from God and it comes and saves the tea's ever-loving soul.)

To my churches throughout the years, so amazing! To Arts Festival! So many lessons learned for me through the years, like learning about how to be a leader to the younger generation!

I am so thankful to have the very best people behind me! To the amazing peeps at HigherLife Publishing & Marketing, Faithe, Andrew . . . you guys are the scratch to that itch right in the center of your back that you can't get on your own. Do you know what I'm talking about? I could *not* have done this without you.

To David, thank you for politely kicking my butt to actually get this book out there. I would still be giving you excuses right now if it wasn't for your foot.

I like y'all, a lot a lot.

REFERENCES

Name: Warren
Relationship: Father
Years Known: Since forever

On July 26, 1990, the Lord blessed Melissa and me with our first baby. A beautiful 9 lb. 11 oz. baby girl who burst onto the scene in the usual dramatic flair she has been known for her whole life. The next day, she was rushed into surgery, and a short time later, we received the most terrifying news any new parent could hear: "Your precious baby daughter has Cystic Fibrosis and it is terminal with no cure. In fact, she most likely will not live to be six years old." This launched us into a perfect storm of fear, anxiety, bewilderment, and for me, guilt. You see, when they told me that it was hereditary, and that both parents had to be carriers, I felt completely responsible. It sounds crazy now, but you have to understand my and Melissa's backstory. I was born into a pretty dysfunctional family with a violent, alcoholic, unfaithful father, and a mother who suffered the effects of the physical abuse and adultery. It was very hard trying to raise three children in a toxic environment, to say the least. Unfortunately, I began to follow in my father's footsteps at an early age.

Eventually I went through drug rehab and the AA and NA 12-step program, and I managed to stay clean my senior year, a miracle in and of itself. Even though sober, I found pornography and sexual relationships as a new addiction and a means of escaping the reality of my internal fears and issues. I became born again right after graduating and soon after that, I joined the Army. I then backslid and ended up getting a girl pregnant. We got married and the Lord blessed me with a wonderful son named Christopher. I ended up using drugs again in Germany and had a horrible experience that landed me in the mental hospital for six months; I was diagnosed with Acute Schizophrenia and medically released from the Army. We moved to Florida and eventually divorced. After a short time in jail, I returned to the Lord and found an awesome church and restored my relationship with God. I ended up meeting Bethany's mother, Melissa, at this time. We began to date and were very active in the ministry of evangelism and drama. Her story was the polar opposite of mine.

She was born again at age five and maintained a faithful and vibrant relationship with the Lord her whole life. The Lord told me at the time that she was the tangible sign of His love for me and that He gave me His very best. She was crazy beautiful, loved Jesus with her whole heart, and had never even had a boyfriend, and the Lord gave her to me as my bride! Soon after we were married, I answered the call to go to the same Bible college that she had graduated from. It was during this time that Bethany was born.

Convinced that her sickness was the direct result of my sinful life, I literally felt like a tornado had touched down in my soul and would not leave. The weight of my guilt was smothering me and overwhelming my ability to even put one foot in front of the other. Not only did I doubt God, but I was angry with Him and was on the brink of completely walking away from it all as I had done before. It was at this time of complete desperation that God intervened. Melissa had stayed with Bethany at the PICU while I went home to grab some things. I walked into the apartment weeping and completely shredded in my soul. All I could say was, "Help me, Lord." I flipped open the Bible, and it landed on the Gospel of John 9:1-3:

> "As He [Jesus] passed by, He saw a man blind from birth. And His disciples asked Him, 'Rabbi, who sinned, this man or his parents, that he would be born blind?' Jesus answered, 'It was neither that this man sinned, nor his parents; but it was so that the works of God might be displayed in him.'"

In that moment, I felt the hand of God come in and hold me up and the peace of God filled my heart. Jesus spoke to the storm in my soul, "Peace, be still." We have stood on that promise Bethany's whole life. When things looked bad, we would just tell ourselves that God was extending her testimony and more people would be there to see "God's works displayed in her." In so many ways she has and is doing just that. She is such an inspiration to so many. I wish I could say that my struggles stopped then, but over the years I have continued to struggle with addictions and selfish living. I regret to say that I have broken my wedding vows many times and went through many battles with mental illness. As Melissa stayed so faithful to the Lord, she had to not only fight for her daughter's health and life but also had to deal with the battle of having an unfaithful and out-of-control husband, fighting to keep her faith strong and not give in to unforgiveness and bitterness toward me.

The only hope we have to hold on to is our faith. We believe that when Jesus died on the cross, He not only offered forgiveness, but also healing. The reality is that my selfish decisions over the years created an environment in our home where fear was tangible, faith was challenged, and forgiveness was absolutely impossible in their own strength. This is why Bethany's story is *so* amazing. In the midst of all of this, she has remained faithful, strong, and full of hope! She and Melissa have been in this fight and bonded so close, not just as mother and daughter, but as prayer partners fighting this spiritual battle together. The Lord blessed us eight years after Bethany was born with our "Tears of Joy": Tearsa Joy. Bethany prayed for a sister and the Lord answered that prayer in a perfect way. I am blessed to say that God has, is, and *will* restore our family.

As Bethany's story continues and *she* lives a life of faith over fear, God is doing amazing things in all of us. We are holding onto His promises and the best *is* yet to come. As He spoke to my heart about a year ago, "Son, I'm fixin' to show off." On that note, as tears stream down my face as I am writing this, I just want to let you know, there is *absolutely* nothing that can keep you from God's love. He is waiting to move into your situation. He is the only cure for our human condition. He can restore, but you have to invite Him in. It's not religion, not church attendance, and not doing enough good to outweigh the bad. Ask God to reveal Himself to you; ask Him to open up your eyes to the reality of His love and the work of the cross! Receive His forgiveness and take hold of the promises He has for you and your family! We are all on this journey together and need each other every day. Fathers, do not let your mistakes and failures drive you away from your children. Children, do not let bitterness, unforgiveness, and resentment for the mistakes of your parents rob you of your relationship with God. God knew what family you were supposed to be born into. Yes, He even knew the things you would suffer and the struggles you would have. You are not a mistake; you were born with a destiny and a purpose. You will find that God will use your battle scars to bring healing to others if you will let Him. Let Jesus take control and your story will continue toward salvation, healing, and wholeness for you and your loved ones!

Name: Melissa
Relationship: Mother
Years Known: Since my womb days

(This portion of the book was dictated by Melissa and typed out by Bethany. Please stand in full agreement with my family that my mother will be restored to perfect health! I am so thankful she was willing and able to tell me all you will read below. My story would not be the same without her input.)

I was saved as a young child and filled with the Holy Spirit at a young age. I grew up praying over my future husband, because I always felt the need to pray for him. I also lifted up my future children. I met Warren at church and instantly fell for his jet-black hair and beautiful, green eyes. We were married and soon we became pregnant and Bethany was on the way. While I was pregnant, many things happened that confirmed this child was going to be special. At one of my early checkups, they told me there was too much fluid around the baby, so they sent me to a specialist. I was praying hard as we went in. They checked me out and asked why they sent me over because there was no extra fluid! A miracle! The last thing I remember was praying for Bethany in my belly one day, and God put the gift of drama on my heart to pray over her. Her father and I were heavily involved in the drama ministry at our church. He would always get the lead roles, and I got the supporting co-star rolls. As I began to pray over her and her gift of drama, I asked that the Lord doubly bless her, more than Warren and me. As I prayed, I felt the Lord say, "Not double, triple anointed." Then I thought, "That's right, because *He* is the third." Boy was this prayer made reality later on in Bethany's life.

When the time came to give birth, Bethany was in my arms after two days of labor. The nurses thought I was crazy for not taking anything to help the pain, because I had been told sometimes the medications can affect the baby. I just prayed through the long labor. Bethany was born around 7 p.m. on July 26, 1990, at 9 lb. 11 oz. When I held her, I told the doctors she felt unnaturally heavy in her middle tummy area. We had our beautiful baby girl for almost twenty-four hours. I had just fed her breast milk and went to the bathroom as Warren burped her. When I came out, Bethany was gone.

Warren told me she had burped up and the nurse told him the color was alarming. We had no idea what was going on, but we began to pray. When the doctor came in, he told us Bethany had to be transported to Baptist Hospital to undergo emergency surgery because of an intestinal blockage. I cried, asking if I could be transported with my baby, but I couldn't since I still needed much rest and recovery. I asked God to watch over Bethany as they let us look at her through the incubator. I put my hands in there and loved on her for the short time I could. As I was asking God to go with her and be there with her, her transport came in to take her, and to our surprise, it was our neighbor from our first apartment! It was like God telling us, "I'm with her," through his familiar face. I had not slept for two days straight, and the doctors and nurses all begged me to try, but I just couldn't. I continued to pray until Bethany was back in my arms. After it all, she was with me, but the big news came later.

After giving her a sweat test, they sat Warren and me down and told us that our baby had Cystic Fibrosis. I remember thinking, "What is that?" They said it was hereditary . . . but we didn't know of anyone in the family who had it. They told us only the basics. It's terminal, and there is no cure. Then they handed me a book telling all about what to expect. I looked at it lying on the table. I heard the Lord say, "Don't read that right now." So I waited to read it. There was a mixture of emotions in that meeting: faith and fear of the unknown. But I just knew my God was not caught off guard by the news like we were. He was in this.

I had a dream one night. In the dream, I was holding Bethany, and she began to shrink and shrivel up in my arms. I was walking through a room full of ministers, well-known preachers, and evangelists. I could tell I was looking for help from them, but wasn't getting noticed. God spoke and said, "I will be the One to heal her." As she grew, she was taught about a healing Jesus who was her most important doctor. Her room had constant worship music playing, and when she was in pain, we would sing her favorite one together. "I am the God, that healeth thee. I am the Lord [Bethany's] healer. You sent your word and healed [Bethany], I am the Lord your healer." I can remember telling her doctors about our expectations for a miracle when she was young, and they saw me praying with a family member. The doctor quickly told me, "If you neglect medication or treatments for this child, I will get her taken from you." My response was quick and without hesitation. I said, "There will come a day when you will test Bethany, and you will see no diagnosis. Until then, I will give her medication, but will always ask about natural help as well." That's what I did. I was her Mommy/Nurse. We believed in doing everything we could to keep her healthy, but we also knew where her healing was going to come from.

When she was a baby, I would have to open up her enzyme pills and pour them into applesauce or jelly. She became sneaky and would swallow the good stuff and line up all the "beads" in between her bottom lip and gum. As a little baby! What a stinker! Bethany had some hospital stays and amazing stories as a young child, but as she grew up, her faith went above and beyond anything I could have hoped for. I am so proud of who she is. When she left our home where all three of us were used to taking care of her and into a marriage with a great young man who had no idea what Cystic Fibrosis meant, it was a hard transition for all of us. But we trusted Jack and Bethany to do all they need to do for her to stay healthy. When she told me about her step of faith, I just had to trust her relationship with Jesus. I know she hears His voice. I have always seen her as healed. "I will reverse the diagnosis" was the word God gave to me when I was praying one day when Bethany was a teenager. I know she is right where she needs to be—in His hands.

Name: Tearsa Joy
Relationship: Sister
Years Known: Since her birth

You would think being almost a decade apart, we would have had trouble getting along. But it was the opposite. We were as close as any two siblings could be. Not only were we each other's entertainment, we were each other's safe place. I can remember countless hours of playing Barbies and coming up with the most ridiculous stories to act out, like always using crazy accents, which I think is where our love of acting and drama came from. Back then we didn't have smartphones, so we had to actually use our imaginations. I can't remember ever having huge fights, although there was that one time I tried to get Bethany to prove her trust in me by letting me leap over her head. We were playing dolls and I had the most brilliant idea. I said, "Sissy, bend down and let me jump over your head!" She was hesitant at first, but with my amazing convincing skills, she agreed. I took a couple steps back (and by a couple, I mean literally to the *back* of our huge playroom) and said, "Here I come!" I started to run and she looked up just in time for her face to get acquainted with my knee. Her nose to be exact. Instantly, a river of blood flowed from her face as well as apologies from my lips, along with many desperate pleas not to tell Mom. Apparently, she didn't accept my apology, because later that same day, she asked me to trust her. Like a complete idiot, I did, and my fate was *far* worse. She coerced me with her charm and "trust me" speech to climb into the empty dryer with nothing but my stuffed cat, Cheddar, in my hands. The dryer door slammed shut and the next thing I knew, I was going through a tumble cycle *with heat!* The only sounds that could be heard were the clanking of my skull on those airplane wings that protrude from the sides and my sister's menacing laugh from outside the door. I was only in there a few tosses, but it felt like an eternity. Needless to say, we were even.

Oddly enough, trust has never been an issue between us. Through hardships growing up, she sheltered me from so many things that I would find out later in life. Her diagnosis of Cystic Fibrosis was never a center point growing up. Honestly, I never remembered she was diagnosed with it until we were at doctor appointments. She was just like any other sibling. She never let it slow her down or stop her from having a fun childhood. As I grew up, I realized it was harder for her to do the normal things that I could every day. I would often wonder why I wasn't born with it too or why it was her instead of me. One time, she even let me try her nebulizer. That was the kind of relationship we had. At around the age of eleven, I understood that she needed care, even to the point where I had to be okay with being overlooked. We didn't glorify CF, but we made sure Bethany's health and happiness remained our main priority. So many China Buffet visits after the doctors, regardless of my begging against it. But I really did understand. I would help out with cooking, patting her back and making her laugh when she was hurting and in pain. That was my favorite part about helping—making her laugh. I even dressed up as a clown when she got out of her surgery. That part has never changed. Even with her last hospital stay, I came up with a funny character and made little videos for her. It always made the stay a little easier for all of us. Out of all her qualities, the one that I always admired the most was her undying faith. She showed me what it really meant to be strong. I never believed that CF would take her life, because that wasn't how we were raised, and we all looked forward to her healing. I wasn't scared of losing her; I just wanted to be there beside her through the good times and bad. Even after she married and left when I was just entering my teen years, we remained the best of friends, and there isn't a thing in the world I wouldn't do for her. I trust her completely. I trust her faith in God 100%. I wish you could see her faith in action like I have. Bethany is definitely a fighter in the spirit but I'm a fighter in the flesh. Mess with her in any way and I'll beat your face and she will pray for your healing.

Name: Chris
Relationship: Brother
Years Known: My whole existence

So, if I'm being honest with myself and everyone, this hasn't been easy to write. I'm not proud to admit it but I'm not as close to my sisters as I should be. All fault and blame for this can be laid at my feet. I was difficult, to say the least, when we were kids. But Bunny, Tearsa, and the family have never made me feel anything other than loved and welcome. My distance had more to do with my relationship with our father when I was younger. I suppose I never really learned or taught myself how to be a good big brother. Admittedly, I'm not really that good at keeping in touch with anyone: friends, family, and the like. Nothing personal at all. I just always seem to find myself engulfed in, well, life.

I do not share the same level of faith as my devout sister and the family she grew up with. Almost all of my experiences with the church were from when I would come visit during the summers. I can say that I certainly value God, and I do believe there is a God. I've seen how His presence positively influences the lives of the people I love and care for. However, I've always struggled with my place in the universe, and my personal relationship with God has always been muddy and confusing at best. But when I see the love and the absolute faith that my sister possesses and how God has held her and guided her through her life, it reminds me that there must be something there. Without fail, Bunny has been through all of her highs and lows holding Jesus' hand. I see how deeply she loves those in her life. I witness how she strives to shape the young minds of tomorrow and I see how difficult life with CF has been for her. I see how she manages to smile through it all, even when I can tell it's not easy. I can imagine that a lot of people with a diagnosis like this might turn bitter or even blame God for it. I know I certainly would. But not our Bunny. If there ever was any doubt within her, she sure handled it well. Her trust and faith are what helps me to not give up on Him in my life. Her unfathomable devotion and utter surrender are to be emulated.

When I heard that she wanted to stop treatment and put it in God's hands, it was hard at first, but I took a moment to process it all and I trusted in her decision. I trust in her trust in God and I have faith in her faith. Now I offer nothing but my absolute support and love moving forward. I'm so proud that I get to call myself her brother.

Name: Kasey
Relationship: Cousin
Years Known: All of them

I have never known a day without Bethany—Bunny to close friends and family. She is my longest-known best friend. Our birthdays are sixty-seven days apart, born cousins but raised more like sisters. We were inseparable growing up, and we did everything together; we even shared the same toilet! This was mostly because she was so small that she couldn't sit on a normal-sized toilet without falling in, so we would sit back-to-back to keep her propped up. We will always have each other's backs, literally and figuratively. Other than being small for her age, she never let anything stop her! As a kid, she was vivacious and active, the entertainer of the family. She would put pencils in her socks and tell everyone that she had leg braces or wear her sunglasses all day at school to convince our first-grade friends that she had suddenly gone blind and wasn't able to do her schoolwork, which somehow she always managed to successfully do. We would put on puppet shows at family gatherings or she would walk around with a fake microphone, interviewing people just for the fun of it.

Growing up with Bunny was anything but boring. It wasn't until we were older that I really understood the day-to-day battle she faced. Imagine not being able to catch your breath, and when you do, it's almost an unbearable pain. Imagine having to take medication every time you ate a meal, or being told that you wouldn't live to see the ages of six, thirteen, twenty-one, or thirty. To most it would make us bitter and say, "Why me?" But not Bethany. She has used what was given to her to encourage others to live a life of faith. Some may scoff at the idea of stopping all medications and treatments that have helped to keep you alive for most of your life and you have never been without. When Bunny told me she was stopping all treatments, I had a moment of fear. Fear that we wouldn't be those hilarious old ladies together as we planned; fear that it would cause her more pain than she already endures; fear that I would have to watch Tearsa grow up without her sister. But fear is *not* what Bunny allows to dictate her life; it is faith, an unshakeable faith even in life's scariest moments. I have never met someone with a faith like hers; it is humbling, inspiring, and often brings tears to my eyes. It's indescribable to watch her go through such painful experiences and continue to keep a steadfast belief in who she is, her faith in God, and her purpose.

Name: Jeweli
Relationship: Close friend
Years Known: Since 2007

I have known Bethany for a *very* long time. I met her back when I was in middle school, and neither of us was as big as a minute! At first, she was just this super-sweet, really funny girl that my older brother had a huge crush on. I never expected her to become one of the most important people in my life. Now I consider her not only a friend, but she's the big sister that I never had.

Throughout the many years of knowing Bethany, there has been one thing that has stood out among all of her other incredible traits. She loves Jesus more than breath itself. It has been hard for me to watch someone with so much faith and life struggle with things that no person should ever have to struggle with. Through the years, I've witnessed Bethany go through not only her physical ailments, but emotional, spiritual, and even family hardships. She has had to endure treatments and hospital stays for weeks at a time; she's been pushed past the breaking point emotionally when all she wanted was to die. Her family has been attacked through mental illness and infidelity, and yet, one thing has remained . . . her will to always remain hopeful and grateful for what God has and will continue to do in and through her life.

I can honestly say that in the 10+ years that I've been a part of Bethany's life, I've never heard a single negative or complaining statement cross her lips. In fact, I've witnessed the complete opposite. When she's stuck in a hospital bed because her body is frail, she'll post videos that bring joy to others. When her family is battling an attack from the enemy, she opens her own home to others who need loving advice or just a comforting shoulder to cry on. I've even had times of struggle and discouragement when, in the midst of her own pain, she has spoken life and encouragement to me.

Bethany is the epitome of what a life pursuing Christ looks like. She has faith that has moved mountains. She has such a grace about her that is humbling. Her spirit is never crushed, and her story has impacted lives too many to count. I have been extremely blessed and honored to have a place in her life. I don't think I will ever know someone quite like Bethany again. She is bold, she is strong, she is talented, and she is a woman with a fire inside of her that has proven to be inextinguishable.

I pray that this book brings awareness and evidence to others that no matter your circumstances, no matter your pain and no matter the number of odds set up against you, with God, you *can* live a life full of joy and peace. Bethany is a living example of this.

Name: Pastor Chris
Relationship: Youth pastor
Years Known: Since 2006

Bright, beautiful, passionate, kind, friendly, energetic, extremely talented, full of faith, and contagious are but a few amazing qualities that describe the life of Bethany. She is one of the most unique individuals I have ever met. Not unique because of these qualities, rather because of the adversity that is Cystic Fibrosis she survives every day while still exhibiting these amazing qualities. I met Bethany when she was a young teenager. She was tenacious and talented. It was a while before I learned of her sickness, because she never let anyone in on her secret battle with CF. She always wanted to be normal and wanted no one feeling sorry for her. Her passion to see a complete healing in her body finally brought her to open up to me and request that I stand with her in prayer and support in witnessing a miracle come to pass. Bethany has never allowed her CF to limit her in any way. Although she's had many stints in the hospital, it has never derailed her ability to write, perform, or coach drama, one of her great passions in life.

A few years ago, Bethany was bedridden at one of our Arts Festival competitions. It was her parents, husband, and I who made her stay in bed, because she does not slow down nor give up. So when coaching from her bed was her only option, she succeeded! From her vision as a young teen about worship encounters with her youth peers to the present day, carrying out her vision in the youth she now mentors—she walks in faith but carries it out in sight. She is an example to all in her belief of God's Word. She doesn't always have answers to tough questions in her own life, but trusts the Lord no matter what! Bethany has been a leader in her family, in her church, in her job, and in the Christian sphere her whole life. Her perspective is always positive and eye-opening. Not only have I been impacted by Bethany's life, but my biological kids and youth kids have been as well. Bethany is one of God's gifts to this planet, and we are all better because of her infectious life. Whether Bethany gets her healing here on earth or in heaven, the testimony of her faith and trust in Jesus will live on forever!

Name: "Uncle" Scott
Relationship: Family friend
Years Known: Whole life

I have known Bethany before there was a Bethany. I have known Bethany's parents long before there was a Bethany. When she was coming, she set her own terms in coming, and so she decided she was going to come late. From that time to now, she has set her own terms, which makes her awesome. Bethany was born with challenges and the thing I love about her is that she has never been afraid of her challenges and has always stepped up and faced them with lots of prayer, love, and support from her family and friends. She always wins. Her whole life, the doctors have always tried to put a timeline on when she was supposed to die. I love it because whenever they say that, I know for a fact that she's going to blow past their timeline. Bethany is very small in stature, but huge in personality, gifting, and love. When she gives you a hug with those skinny arms, they will hurt you, but you don't mind; she's just that powerful. I love her power because she loves slapping the devil around and being a thorn in his butt. He keeps trying to kill her, but God keeps protecting her and she keeps laughing in the devil's face. Her life has been full of challenges, but her life still has much more to go because God is not done with Bethany. He's going to use her powerfully as a reminder to everyone that the devil is a loser and that no matter what any man or any devil says . . . God makes you a winner. She is a winner.

Since Day One,
God's Been in This

The first miracle happened the day I was born. Coming from a mother and grandmother who were both premature at birth, weighing only about five pounds, you can imagine my mother's surprise when I was born a whopping 9 lb. 11 oz.! My birth was normal, despite being the size of a toddler and coming out wanting a steak, I'm sure. Things took a turn for the worst when my father was holding me and I began to throw up the breast milk I had just drank. The nurse quickly took me from my parents, and I was rushed into emergency surgery. They told my parents it was a case of meconium ileus, which is when the baby's first stool is thicker than normal and blocks the last part of the small intestine. Mine had not only blocked up my small intestines, it had become crystallized. They cut a chunk of the small intestine and also took out my appendix while they were at it, leaving a scar which is still numb and often causes a traffic jam during the digestion process. (Fun Fact: Confused, I used to say they took out my pancreas till I was like twenty and my mom heard me say it and was like, "What?" So funny.)

Sounds more like a tragedy than a miracle, but since I was born such a large baby, I could undergo surgery easier. But it gets even better. When the operation was over, they watched me closely to ensure my recovery. In that time, they ran what is known as a sweat test. Then the doctors had to deliver some news that I can only describe as "the frightening unknown." My mother and father were told that their child had an incurable, terminal disease called Cystic Fibrosis (CF). My father took the news way harder because they were told it was a genetic condition. People with CF have inherited two copies of the defective CF gene—one copy from each parent. People with only one copy of the defected CF gene are carriers but do not have the disease themselves. My parents had no idea they were carriers. In fact, we can't find the disease on either side, but, of course, CF had been misdiagnosed as many other similar conditions in the past, such as asthma. About 25% (1 in 4) of children born to two carriers will have CF. So, you could say, this was a case of *What in the world!*

My father's testimony was the exact opposite of my mother's. After God revealed to him His plan in all this, John 9:1-3 was a go-to passage in times of trial. With any health battle from then on, that word was *peace* to my father and eventually to me. (Author's Addition: When you're walking in a battle where you are standing in faith for your child, listen for the words from God. Write them down, teach them and instill them into your child, and they will form a foundation for them to build their faith on. The words God gave to my parents throughout my life were fuel to my faith as I grew up.) The doctors offered my parents a book on what to expect and said that my life expectancy was not long. Of course, my parents did not accept this as my fate. They began to stand on God's Word and declare my healing.

They took their little baby home and only a few weeks went by before I began throwing up my mother's milk again, and she noticed very thick mucus in my nose and throat. She brought me to the doctors, and they immediately noticed my weight loss due to the throwing up. After the doctors looked in my nose, they were floored by how congested I was. They began IV antibiotics and started me on a high-calorie formula instead of my mother's milk. No weaning me off, just switching completely. I began to throw it up, not wanting the nasty formula. I know it's nasty because my mother used to taste everything before making me take it, because she is the best mother ever, and she told me it was awful.

My mother watched me lose a little more weight as she desperately tried to get me to eat the formula. The doctor labeled me a "failure to thrive," and after that, my mother breastfed me, then prayed and said, "Now she will take the formula like it was my milk." And I did. Again, if I had been born a small baby, the weight loss would have been detrimental.

I was released from the hospital as soon as my congestion cleared up, and things were . . . normal. I was gaining weight and my lungs were unbelievably clear. Things were great, other than the sunflower mishap of 1992, where I found my father's seeds with the shell on in his work bag and managed to shove a bunch down the hatch before my mother found me. After a short trip to the hospital, consisting of an X-ray (showing serious blockage) and a powerful enema, and an entire church family praying for me to have a serious bowel movement, things were back to normal. My parents placed me around other children growing up at the church nursery, play dates at our little apartment, eventually school and even ballet classes. Cystic Fibrosis was only one part of my life.

At three years old, we had our next miracle when we encountered one of the least pleasant symptoms of CF called a rectal prolapse, a condition in which the rectum—the last part of the large intestine before it exits the anus—loses its normal attachments inside the body, allowing it to telescope out through the anus, thereby turning it "inside out." Ouch, right? When this happened for the first time, my parents were a bit taken aback. To quote Dad's words, "What the heck is that?" They pulled that book out and began to read about it. They called my doctors, who told them step by step how to push it back into place. Now, I may have been only three when this started happening, but I promise you, I remember the pain and the thick, white carpet I would cry into as I laid across my dad's crisscrossed legs on the bathroom floor as he had to slowly push it back inside me. I cried so badly it would make them cry. I'm so thankful to say this only happened a total of three times, because here comes my first victory as a prayer warrior. At around four years old, I went into the bathroom on my own and told my mother I wanted to pray and sing worship songs while I went. After experiencing such a scare and such pain, and each trip to the bathroom held the possibility of it happening again, it was scary to go. My mother waited on the other side of the door, singing with me, and after a while I came out and said, "Mommy, Jesus put it back, and it's never going to happen again." We rejoiced and believed it, and you know what? It never happened again.

I can remember going to many doctor visits at a young age, and like the Groundhog Day film, it was the same routine each time: weigh in, sit on paper, look into my father's ears and nose with the equipment on the walls, and cringe at the doctor's cold stethoscope. Mother would often tattle on

4

me for not wanting to take my enzymes with every snack and the doctor would give me "that look." I would sit in the see-through box with the nose plug tighter than my lips could be around the mouthpiece as I would breathe in and out normally for three counts. Then, my heart would pick up as my respiratory therapist would cheer me on to breathe out: "Longer, longer, longer, push, push, push. And when you have nothing left, deep breath in." Then at the end, we would head up three floors to the dreaded lab. I would sit on my father's lap and turn my head away from the nurse, and my father would whisper about all the delicious, weird foods we were going to eat at the China Buffet as soon as it was over.

This was CF to me. This was as bad as it got. But this was not normal for CF patients, especially those diagnosed as early as I was. I know that's all credit to God and to my parents for never making CF my identity, even to the point of teaching me to say, "I was diagnosed with Cystic Fibrosis," never "I have Cystic Fibrosis." They would tell me, "We do not say you have it because it has no right to be in your body." I am so thankful for the environment of faith my parents raised me up in. My mother would play worship music in my bedroom, and we would sing our favorite songs together when I had any pain. What a great foundation of faith. Some would say I was sheltered growing up, which I guess when you look at the fact that I only watched Christian cartoons every now and then and all my friends were from private school and church (which were usually the same friends because my private school was often at my church) . . . yeah, I may have been sheltered. But I was often found getting myself in unique situations. I like to call this part . . .

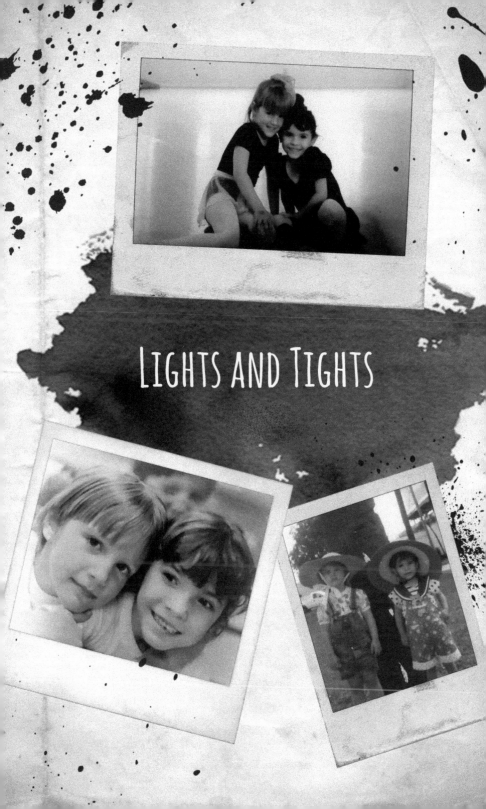

Lights and Tights

At a very young age, my flair for the dramatic could not be overlooked. At the age of three, we watched a cartoon (Christian, of course) and I asked my mother to act it out with me. I said my lines, and she tried to say hers, but her voice sounded like Mom and not like the character. So I corrected her mistake and even did the voice for her so she could repeat it the right way. It still wasn't perfect, so I had to do it all on my own, with multiple characters' lines, actions, and voices. Mom watched amazed and started feeling strongly that this was a sign of the gift God had placed in me which she prayed for when I was in her belly. She and my father did drama ministry at their church, he always getting the lead roles and even writing some of the lines, and her being the supportive co-star when needed. There is a photo from a drama performance where she was on stage and there I was, a huge 9 lb. baby inside her tummy—posing for the picture no doubt.

I had the inner burnings of a performer—or a really convincing liar, depending on how you looked at it. School was always the best place to show off my acting skills. Once I acted like I was blind and persuaded my neighbor beside me to do my work because, well, I couldn't see it. I kept it going for a while until my cousin, Kasey, walked in the room as a new student and was seated directly in front of me, getting herself a front row seat to my award-winning performance. I tried to come up with a plan, but I wasn't as fast as the loudmouth who had been doing my work; she introduced me as her blind friend Bethany. Kasey was not one to play along with my games—ever—and was quick to call me out on my lie. Back to doing my work on my own. Better luck next time.

Another time, we were heading to PE, my least favorite part of the day. Our uniforms at the private school required knee-high socks, which I hated. Usually I would get in trouble for rolling them down. I had a great idea; I stuffed several pencils in my socks on both sides of my ankle and started walking with a bad limp. This academy-award winning performance got me out of running laps . . . that day.

Quickly, I found my place in the senior class production as the only cast member who was not a senior. *Jailhouse Rock* was the first time I set foot on a stage as an actress. I had a solo! I was in love.

The next time I was seen on stage was during the school play, *The Sound of Music,* with less flattering roles such as "baby goat" and "child with lollypop at the party." But I loved it anyway! My mother got me into ballet classes with the most amazing teacher who had a soft spot in her heart for my bulging tummy in that pink leotard—not to mention sweatbands around my head and limbs because I had to be extra. Mrs. Lori was often giggling at my cuteness too much to notice that I could almost never plié big enough to go over the fake puddles on the floor. I loved ballet class and, of course, having my sidekick and personal lie detector, Kasey, in it with me made it better.

I must mention my greatest performance, which was during *The Prince of Egypt.* There was a spontaneous worship part where everyone in our company, old and young, came on the stage and danced an un-choreographed number. I had gone to the restroom right before we went on and had misplaced my skirt, and no one could stop me from running up and doing the "funnest" dance where I was free! Free to express myself. I was doing my thing! Dancing in the blinding lights, showing off all I knew about ballet. Kasey began to annoy me because she kept getting in between me and the audience. As I noticed she was doing this on purpose, it became a fight of who could be seen more. Keep in mind, we were on a stage full of other dancers, all worshiping.

Eventually, I looked over to the right of the audience, and through the blinding lights I could see my aunt cracking up and my mother and great-grandma looking very shocked. The lights went off and we headed backstage, where my cousin explained that her annoying upstaging had a purpose. When the lights would hit just right, my leotard was totally visible through my flesh-colored, stretched tights. I never questioned Kasey's motives again. She has always had my back. (Fun Fact: My skirt was in plain sight backstage, sitting by the bathroom.)

I couldn't help but spice up my life; it was the writer in me that eventually would come out in a good, constructive way. My cousin has story after story of me "practicing" my skills on her.

My family went through difficult times as I grew up, but I was sheltered from a lot of it as a young child. You would never have guessed, because we didn't let everyone into our intimate struggles as a family. I have no memories of split-ups or arguments at all as a young child. I do remember being confronted with the fact that my father had been married before to another woman, and that was hard to understand. But I was excited because I had a brother. There was no *half*-brother nonsense; he was my Bubba. He came when I was really young, and I can only remember that time through pictures and videos. He was so funny! He was always making me laugh, and he played the older brother role perfectly. We didn't look alike at all because he was half Thai, so he was way tanner than all of us. He would go from an only child with his mother to big brother when with us. No matter how much I loved having a brother around the house, he was a stranger to me, because we never got the time together to really develop a relationship.

Around the time he left, my parents announced they were pregnant. This was great news! I had begged and prayed for a little sister for a long time, so I just knew this was her! I was eight when my little sister, Tearsa Joy, was born. My mother had to be rushed to the hospital in the middle of the night, and I was left with our neighbors. I guess I was a deep sleeper because I wasn't aware of anything until I woke up in their house. They called my parents and I was able to talk to my sister for the first time. They put the phone near her, and I said, "Hey sissy!" They said she opened her eyes wide and screeched with joy! This was what I had been praying for. We grew up matching (by force), playing dolls, embarking on wild, imaginary adventures, and eventually going through difficult times hand-in-hand. We also had a tendency to get a little rowdy and carried away. Like the time I put her in the dryer and turned it on, because she decided to try and jump over my head and busted my nose. Blood was everywhere!

There were also really odd moments in our lives that we had nothing to do with; they just happened to us like the plot in a sitcom. Like the time we finally got a slip-n-slide, and the raccoons got to it first. We literally watched them play and then tear it all to pieces. There was also the time we went exploring in our backyard and found an upside-down pickup truck with a garbage bag beside it in the distinct shape of a body, but it was gone by the time any adults came to see it. I finally had someone to share all my creativity with. We loved Barbies and could play for hours, creating story after story. When the difficult times came, she was kept from them just as I was when I was young. The only problem was that you can't hide things forever.

Pretty soon, Cystic Fibrosis began to rear its long-overdue head for all of us to confront face-to-face, completely unprepared. Up to that point, it had just been in the background. At sixteen, I got just a taste of what real CF was like. I had been putting off a much-needed sinus surgery for a few years. I became used to not being able to breathe through my nose, and little did we know that this growth, which is called a polyp, had become so big that it blocked my entire right nostril and had pushed my septum over to close up about 80% of my left nostril. I went in to go over surgery plans, and my doctors told me I would need a "tune-up" before they operated. What is a tune-up? I had no idea, but it's a familiar CF term meaning hospitalization for generally two weeks, where they hit treatments hard and try to get both lung function and weight gain up and harmful lung bacteria growth down! By sixteen, many patients would have had several of these tune-ups. I didn't know what to expect, and this really didn't fit into my plans of being a super-awesome teenager. But my family—yes, all four of us—packed our bags and headed to the hospital to face the unknown. My family walked with me through these moments. I can remember looking over and seeing my father sleeping in the little chair in the corner and my mother and sister on the little couch by the window. They refused to let me walk through this alone, and I'm beyond thankful for each of them.

At this point, I wasn't taking anything more than enzymes during my snacks and meals. In the hospital, I was introduced to the procedures that come with the tune-up title. First, nebulizers! I had only taken a nebulizer a few times my whole life (only simple treatments such as albuterol and hypertonic saline), but they were going to introduce me to some nebulized antibiotics. Next, IV antibiotics to ensure that any infections that might be camping out and growing a village in the lungs are gone. This is where I learned I wasn't about to just get a normal IV. I was told that a PICC line was the way they liked to do things. You could tell they were used to this being totally normal for CF, but it was very scary to me. I started bawling and freaking out. After much convincing from my CF team that this was the best route, they told me we needed to get it done. But it was not okay with me until they brought out the "happy juice." My father explains it like this: "You went into the bathroom scared and crying, then when you came out, you busted the door wide open and said so confidently, 'Let's do this thing!'" Apparently, while under the influence, I also made the PICC nurse laugh while

I was getting it placed, and she told my daddy she had never laughed during a placing before. With the PICC placed, all that's left to do was wait and let your body tune up. (See what I did there?)

For two weeks straight, I was stuck in a frustrating routine of being awakened and poked up by needles for lab work the moment I fell asleep. Then when I would finally go back to sleep, I would be awakened again for my nebulizer treatments. I had to eat nasty meals, all the while hoping the next one would be better but nope . . . but maybe the next one . . . nope. I kept questioning myself, "Why do I keep hoping it gets better just to be disappointed?" I would have surprise visitors come in, and I would have to act like I was happy to see them, but really, I was mortified because I hadn't showered in a couple days, and I looked like a drugged raccoon (because of the lack of sleep, dark circles surrounded my eyes).

After all that, and after all the guilt I felt for my family members swapping out from time to time and sleeping on a plastic couch and an uncomfortable chair just so I didn't have to be alone, it was finally time for my surgery. With the PICC line in for its last assignment, I was about to be wheeled back to the operating table. They brought out the much-needed happy juice and I instantly, upon administration, felt like breaking out into song. I kissed my family goodbye and laughed while (I thought) blurting out the weirdest quotable lines I could think of that would have made great "last words" as they pushed my wheelchair through the passage to all things bright and sanitary. Actually, my last words were far less likely to make it onto a T-shirt. "*Hey guys*! This looks like a kitchen. Are you guys going to chop me up and cook meahhhhhhhahgsfuagifgu?"

I woke up in recovery and started whimpering because the happy juice was long gone, and there was intense pressure in my head. I had a moment of vulnerability where I felt entitled to feel sorry for myself. Through my tears, I looked to my right, and there was a young boy looking at me. He asked me, "Are you okay?" I started crying harder, telling him how bad my nose hurt, how sore my throat was, and how much I needed a drink. Then I asked him why he was back there. He told me, "I just had open heart surgery." Insert awkward silence and a few shared stares and blinks. I didn't say another word to that superhuman of a child beside me. I kept my wimpy whimpers internalized, trying to act tough.

After I recovered, they sent me home with my PICC line and a supply of antibiotics. I was told to return in a few weeks for a follow-up surgery, which I really dreaded. The at-home treatment wasn't easy either. Needing to trust my parents to flush my PICC line without getting any air in it had me stressed to the max, and of course, trying to maneuver through everyday life with one arm was far from easy. I was beyond ready to get that thing out.

The time came to get my PICC removed, and it went as good as it could have gone. But then the surgery came, and it was very different from the first time on the chopping block. They started with the happy juice, but this time, instead of putting it through my PICC line—which had an instant effect—they gave it to me orally. I took it . . . and nothing happened, at all.

They assured me it would kick in, but not soon enough. I begged for more time, and they told me it was time to go back to the operating room. "Wait a minute! I'm not happy! Stop! *No!*" This was the tune I was singing, which was very different from last time. I was brought through the double doors into the "kitchen" feeling as normal as can be. They put me up on the table while I continued letting them know that I was feeling very much myself and was not ready for this. Then they put the gas mask on me, and they asked me to count backwards from ten. I got to nine and then experienced a strange series of events. I woke up in recovery and the strange events continued, as my sister was dressed up like a clown dancing at the foot of the hospital bed and I was trying to figure out if I was really awake just yet.

After my surgery and my first tune-up, they decided it would be best to begin nebulizing every day. So, at sixteen years old, I began the normal Cystic Fibrosis relationship with the dreaded nebulizer-time-consumer. This would begin the treatments that would end up being two hours long each day of my life for the next twelve years. That's 730 hours a year and a total of 8,760 hours in twelve years, which adds up to an entire year of my life hooked to a nebulizer just breathing. But at sixteen years old, just as my body had begun taking the form of a Cystic Fibrosis patient, I had a dream that would change my life.

Is She Dead?

To understand this dream, I have to take you back to me being nine years old. I was asked to come over and stay the night with one of my distant aunts to help watch my cousin. As a family, we were almost always together, and I was rarely seen without them. Even though I wasn't so attached to them that I would crawl into their beds or anything (in fact, I loved having my own room and space), I never stayed the night anywhere else because I liked having them close enough to me if I needed them. (This was before any big health scares, so things were pretty much normal.)

I went to my aunt's house to stay, and the atmosphere was so different from what I was used to. Sounds crazy that even at nine I could sense the difference, but it felt so foreign to me. I felt unsafe, as if I had stepped into a stranger's house, even though it was my aunt. I knew she did not have the same morals as my family, but she was still someone who would have done anything to protect me. Her husband, my uncle, was playing a game with monster trucks, and I remember an ugly clown face being painted on the side of it. Then I noticed my uncle was drinking. This was something I had never been around. Even though he did not get drunk that night and never made any remarks or did anything that may have led me to believe he was, I remember feeling uncovered and completely unsafe. I knew he was the head of the home, and he was my protection while I was under his roof.

The time came to go to bed. My aunt could tell I was uneasy and told me I could stay up and watch as many Disney movies as I wanted with my little cousin. I tried to keep her awake to watch them with me so I wouldn't be alone, but she fell asleep. That's when I decided I couldn't pretend I was okay any longer. I went into the living room, got the house phone, and went into my cousin's closet because I was scared and embarrassed. My father answered the phone and just hearing his voice brought me to tears. I missed them so much and the safety I felt with them. I felt alone in the world in that closet, surrounded by darkness with just the feelings of being so far away from safety. I felt like God Himself was left at my house and didn't come with me. I hung up the phone and kept reminding myself, "Daddy and Mommy will be here soon."

I remember that moment in the dark as if I were still there. I felt such a heaviness push me until my head was literally on the floor. A heavy pressure on me. I just laid there in a puddle of tears, waiting. I had experienced fear before, but never like this. You can imagine my relief when I heard my parents and my baby sister pull up in the car. I held them tight and made up my mind that I was never leaving home again, ever.

That's when a spirit of fear attached itself to me, and we began our addictive, abusive relationship. I would often feel like I couldn't escape. Later through life, I would have moments of severe separation anxiety, as some would call it, but it was just fear. I actually chased my parents down the road once, begging them to not leave me at the house when they just needed to run up the road for something, and I was thirteen. There were times when my parents would have to make arrangements to come with me on overnight events such as church camps. Then I had to use my storytelling skills and come up with a reason they were with me, because I couldn't be honest and tell people I was scared to be alone. Fear had a tight grip on me, and it created bondage not only for me, but my family felt the effects as well, which is why it is such a common and powerful tool of the devil. My husband has told me that feeling scared is part of being human, but being in fear is a choice. My father once had a dream of a loved one being in a cage and the key was right beside them. Fear is like that—totally unnecessary bondage that you don't have to live in.

Now, we can return to the dream. My family and I had just started going to the church that would play such a vital role in my life. At sixteen, the pressure to fit in was huge! I went to my first youth service, and it felt like high school. Everyone had their friends, and I was clearly not noticed by them. I was totally fine with sitting in the very back and sneaking out early to avoid being the awkward new kid. I did that once, then the next service came and I said to myself, "I'm going to be coming here for a long time, and I need friends." Boldness came over me, and I jumped in the center of every clique and introduced myself! Then I sat alone in the back because no one asked me to sit with them. The next service I had several offers, and that started some friendships which are still going to this day.

My youth group had this event they would do periodically called the Worship Encounter. Everyone kept asking me to go, and I really wanted to, but . . . it was a stay-the-night thing. Thinking about being away from my parents made my hands sweat and my heart flutter, but I wasn't about to tell my new friends that I was a chicken. So, I would come up with excuses. The obvious excuse that no one would question would be, "Because of my medications, it would be too much of a hassle." But that wasn't an option for me because I told no one about Cystic Fibrosis except for my pastors, and I asked them to please not say anything about it because I did not want to be known for CF. So, I would usually lie, saying I was busy or something. This weighed heavy on my heart and I wanted to go so badly. My fear was holding me back and I was letting it. Then I had a dream . . .

It started with a church bus pulling up in front of me. The bus doors opened, and one of my youth pastors, Pastor Chris, was driving. He called for me to get on. I tried to step on, but couldn't. I looked down, and I saw a ball and chain attached to both of my feet. Pastor Chris said, "Pick it up and come on." So, I did. When I got to my window seat, I began to feel fear. Yes, it has a distinct feeling which I know well. I looked out the window, and my family was there, waving and smiling at me. I panicked and debated running off and going to them, but instead, I forced a fake smile and waved back. Instantly, I was in a gym, but not the one at my church that I knew. It was one I'd never seen before. My youth worship team was singing on the stage, and the entire youth group was worshiping. Then I saw me . . . worshiping. I was confused at first because there was such a feeling of reality in this dream that I thought I was really there. Were there two of me? Very weird! I began watching like I was in a movie. Beside me was a tall, bright being. I couldn't make out any features, but I knew it was a heavenly figure. I looked back to me in the crowd and both of my youth pastors came up on each side of me. They took my hands, and Pastor John asked me, "Are you ready?" I said, "Yes." Then everyone began to pray for me. Everyone in the whole room moved closer to me, and they had their hands on me or on those in front of them.

Instantly, I was outside of the gym at a fire pit, and one of the youth leaders was carrying wood to the fire. The trees started to sway, and a wind came. Then the most amazing sight happened, and I got to see it. Out of the sky, directly above the gym, came a tunnel of light. It made a big boom, and when it hit the gym roof, a big gust of wind came, and it was so strong it knocked the leader over. Then I was on the gym roof, able to stick my head inside the light tunnel and look down through the roof. It was around me and my pastors, and we were not even acting like we saw it. We were still praying with our eyes closed. I looked up into the tunnel, and it was filled with streaks of beautiful colors. I felt the wind generated from the tunnel's spinning.

Instantly, I was back in the gym, standing in the back looking at myself in the middle of this light tunnel. There was a huge demon with his claws dug into my shoulders, hanging onto my back with his feet around my waist. I looked at the shining being that had been beside me this whole time. Neither of us had spoken to each other until that point. I said to it, "That must be Cystic Fibrosis" (meaning infirmity and sickness). The being said, "No, that's the demon of fear. Your fear is bigger than your sickness." That was the only thing this being said to me. I then looked back at myself, and the demon turned and looked at me, and FEAR was engraved in its forehead. I looked around the room, and it was full of demons attached to my youth group, all with their titles engraved somewhere on their bodies. I wasn't able to see what demon was attached to what person because God didn't want me to, and I'm glad. I had many friends in that room.

As the praying continued, a loud noise happened again, and it was as if another layer of light came over the first one. This created a wind-type surge, and the demons were forced off a little but were still holding on. Then, out of the light came shards of sharp, piercing light that impaled the demons and pinned them to the gym wall. I had to jump out of the way of the fear that was coming right at me. When the demons hit the wall, they disappeared. As I looked at myself, my body became transparent. I saw my lungs being made whole, my pancreas beginning to work, and my digestive system being restored to its proper order. I watched myself be healed. Then as the light left, going right back up as it had come, everyone was out in the Spirit. I waited a long time in the gym, walking around looking at everyone closely. I noticed light coming from parts of their bodies, such as their eyes and fingers. Finally, they all began to wake up, everyone but me. I followed as they carried me to the girls' bunks, and as about five of my girlfriends were around me, I became the Bethany on the bed they were looking at. I heard one ask, "Is she dead?" Then I opened my eyes and looked at them. That was the end of it. (Author's Addition: I don't know how to explain it, but through the years, this dream has changed in my memory. It's almost like deeper revelation has been birthed through the years I have thought on it, shared it, and believed God for it. I know this because I recently found a diary of mine where I wrote this dream a few years after I had it. Certain people changed and the details would change, but it always held the same overall message, which was me being healed.)

I woke up, told my family, wrote it down and placed it in a special little box of mine on top of my dresser. I know this sounds like some crazy stuff, but I went to get the paper and it was gone. I wrote it again, placed it in the box, and it disappeared again. I had this dream a total of three times, the exact same dream, every detail. I realized it was okay that I couldn't look back over the paper, because I could, and still can, remember every single detail of that dream. This gave me much hope. It also had a lot of answers I had been praying about. When you are believing God for a healing and you're not seeing it, people will assume you are doing something wrong. But the Bible says, "By his stripes we are healed" (Isa. 53:5 NKJV). God is no respecter of persons. What He has done for one, He will do for many. Continue to press in and believe for your healing. No matter what things look like, speak by faith. Do not give up praying for it.

My parents never made me feel like I wasn't healed because of my own failures. They always told me I was healed at the cross, and we would believe it and speak it before we saw it, because it was done. It took some time for me to tell Pastor Chris about the dream. I described all I saw, and he said that was the retreat property the church owned where they would take the youth for the Worship Encounters. That was really a confirmation that it was from God because I had never been there, but he described it perfectly. They had already decided on not doing the Worship Encounters anymore, and I was glad because I didn't want to face that fear. I know you might be thinking, "That's crazy. That's where you would be healed. Why do you not want that?" It's because fear was driving my emotions, and I allowed it to dictate all my decisions.

Through my life, God would continue to use dreams as a way of communicating with me. But now we are coming to the part of my story that almost was my end, *but God*. I call this . . .

Stop Being Selfish! It's Not About You!

A t eighteen, I was happy with my life. I was involved with an Arts Festival program at my church. I had a best friend, and I was heavily involved with my youth group. Life was going pretty well. Then around December 2008, I went in for my regular doctor's appointment, feeling normal. They put the X-ray up on the illuminator and pointed out a tiny spot in one of my lungs that looked like a blip. Now, I have to tell you about my doctor. He literally always had a smile on his face. That's fine if you are being told good news, but being told bad news with a smile makes you want to punch his teeth out.

Anyway, so he said (with a big, dumb smile), "We think this is pneumonia." Meaning it must not be that bad to not even know for sure. Being completely new to this being sick stuff, I asked what oral antibiotics they were going to give me. He said (with a smile), "That's not how it works with Cystic Fibrosis. We are going to admit you into the hospital and give you a PICC line for your IV medications." I was a mess. I had so many questions. Why does it have to be this extreme if it's so small? Why do I feel normal? Why are you smiling like that? No answers, just, "This is how we do it with CF." I was admitted right away, a PICC line was placed, and the medications began. I was only in there long enough to refresh my parents on how to do the care that comes with at-home treatments.

When I was released, from day one, everything went wrong. The at-home nurse came and helped my daddy with the first hook-up. As soon as the clamp was undone and the medication began to go in, I projectile vomited all over the kitchen and blacked out. I woke up on the couch, and my line was being cleaned. I was asked how I felt. I didn't have an answer. I had no idea what just happened. It was the same medication I had been on just a few hours before.

Because there are so many mutations, there are many differences within the CF community. What helps one patient can make the other have horrible reactions and side effects and do little good. Also, a medication that has worked for a patient in the past can begin to not work at all because the bacteria has become resistant. This means the medication needs to be stronger or a new medication needs to be tried.

As a patient grows up, going through multiple hospitalizations and medications, their list of antibiotics dwindles down, and the doses remain very potent, leading to many issues such as kidney failure, failing immune systems, and a lot of blown veins because of the harshness of the antibiotics. However, I came into the game so late that almost all the antibiotics worked for me. The bacteria in my lungs were susceptible to them, and they didn't have to be really strong doses because my body had not been learning to fight them all these years. So, when they would prescribe me medications, the doctors would make assumptions about the required strengths because I was a Cystic Fibrosis patient in my teens, and sometimes the medications were too strong and I would have a negative reaction.

Anyways, back to me on the couch. The nurse changed how fast the antibiotics were flowing into my line and that helped. Now that I was in the comfort of my own home, away from all the doctors and my church family, where I had to act like I had it all together, I broke, and I broke hard. (Author's Addition: If my life were a movie, this part of my life would be what I showed you in the trailer. However, like my dream where I told you the details changed, the details changed with these events as well, making me realize that His words to me in certain seasons are what I need for that exact time, and as the seasons change, new perspective may come from that word He spoke, or I will no longer remember something because I wasn't meant to bring it into a new season with me. I'm not saying this is how it works for everyone, but this is how I have seen Him work in me.) I had always been so hopeful, full of joy and faith. It was during this time I started seeing that I wasn't normal at all, and it was basically like receiving an eviction notice from your body without warning, telling you, "Dear Bethany, you have a terminal disease out of nowhere, and you are starting to feel your body take it on as your long-overdue identity. You will no longer be able to hide from others, because this is your fate. You drew the short straw in life, and your body is going to kill you little by little, and the treatments, no matter how harsh, and no matter how convincing and hopeful the doctors try to be about them, won't save you. Welcome to Cystic Fibrosis . . . good luck. Love, your body."

My mother was going through some health complications of her own during this time, but she never for a minute let me feel alone in my fight. I was in the lowest place I had ever been—so low I entertained the thought of suicide. I was in my room between antibiotics, and I was just sitting on my bed. My father came in and knew I was not myself, so he tried to get me to open up to him, but he left after I begged him to just leave me alone, reassuring him that I was fine. I took a syringe and filled it with air. I knew it would kill me, with the PICC being so close to my heart and having seen how they would make sure no air was in my line. I remember feeling numb, and I wasn't even crying; I was just angry and numb. I hooked the syringe to my PICC, unclamped my line and began to slowly push.

Before the air could go into my vein, my neighbor, Noah, who I had grown up with, came to my bedroom window, which was open. He must have pushed through all the bushes in front of it. He said, "Bethany, let me in." I hid what I was doing in embarrassment, and because his surprise visit had me more curious than anything, I unhooked my line and walked out to the front door. When I opened it, Noah came in and just gave me this hug I will never forget. He held me for a while, then he looked at me and said, "I just had to come tell you I love you." I was shocked at the timing of all this, but deep down, I knew it was orchestrated by God. Noah grabbed a popsicle, like he always did, and left. (Fun Fact: Years later, at a wedding, I finally told Noah what his surprise visit to my window stopped me from doing. He told me that never happened. I argued with him, explaining all the facts, and he still told me it was not him. My mother and sister were my witnesses that Noah did visit us that day. Since he had no memory of this event, I am convinced that it was an angel sent in the form of the only person who could have come to my window with it seeming normal and safe to hug him.) Thinking back on it, I can't help but cry. I'm so thankful for that intervention which saved my life. But my battles were just beginning. I tried so many ways to give up. Within one week, I experienced both God and the devil in a whole new way—like an extreme spiritual warfare kind of way.

My next step in giving up was just being swallowed up with self-pity. I was standing in the kitchen with my mother, and her eyes caught mine, and it felt as if I was completely weak. "I just want to . . ." is all I could get out before I collapsed into her arms, and she said, "Don't you say it." She held me as I cried violently on her shoulder. As I was crying, my vision turned totally black, but for whatever reason I didn't freak out. I began to see many faces in front of me. Some I knew. Some I had never seen before. I heard God's voice. He said, "Stop being selfish! It's not about you! If you can't hold on for yourself, hold on for them." The faces continued as if I was watching a slide-show presentation. Just as the last act of God did, this gave me the strength to fight another day.

The next day, I felt such depression, which I had never felt before or since, thank God. I laid on the couch in our family living room, and I honestly made up in my heart and mind that there must not be a God. How can He allow me to suffer like this? Again, I was only focusing on the current pain I was in and not even thinking or remembering all the many, many times God had His hand on me, including just the day before. So, as I looked up at the ceiling, I said from my heart, "I don't believe in You."

Instantly, my eyes became shut to where I couldn't open them, and my arms felt like they were fastened to each side. But then, the craziest thing happened. It felt as if someone was sitting on my chest, holding me by the collar of my shirt. Then they pulled my upper body up and slammed it down, not hitting the back of my head on the couch but slamming it on the arm rest of the couch. (Unfortunately, there was very little fabric over the wood framing.) This happened several times, and I couldn't do anything, not even scream. Even though this was an obvious attack of the devil, I was still so angry that I didn't want to cry out to God to save me.

What I believe I was experiencing was God's hand of protection—which had been placed over me at birth and kept over me all my life— being lifted from me because of my confession of unbelief. As soon as that covering was lifted, the devil came immediately to take me out. As this was happening, I finally could let out a scream. My parents rushed in and began to pray over me. There was no damage to the back of my head like there would have been if that attack physically happened, and they never heard or saw anything to prove it happened. But I was living it; it was all spiritual. Looking back, it freaks me out, because it was really happening to me! I felt it. This wasn't the only time something like that would happen.

After that mess, the last attempt to give up came the next morning. My parents had moved me into their bed. I was lying next to my father, just looking at the ceiling, as warm tears fell down my face into my ears. My faith in God was back, of course, but I didn't have anything left in me. I felt worn out from the physical, emotional, and spiritual breakdowns I had just walked through. Now, I just wanted to wave the white flag of surrender to God. As I was thinking it, my father asked me what I was thinking about. I said, "I just need to go." He thought I was talking about going back to the hospital, but then I told him I wanted to go to heaven. We had a special moment where I looked into his eyes, and he must have felt my pain because he didn't try to argue with me. He simply closed his eyes as they filled with tears, and I turned back to looking at the ceiling and told God I was ready to go. There comes a point when the only way you can help a person is through prayer. When someone is ready to truly give up, no one but God can save them. That is why it's so important that we uplift and encourage each other every chance we get. You would never want the last thing you said to someone to be anything but loving. Treat everyone like it's their last day; speak life to those around you.

In that moment, I saw five angels coming toward me from a distance. It freaked me out. There were no heavenly harps or me walking slowly into the light; I had asked for something I was completely unprepared for. I shot up really quick and said, "Never mind! I'm not ready yet!" In that moment, God gave me a milestone word. He said, "I love you enough to take you if it hurts too bad." Wow. That was it. The battling was done. I had a new perspective. God had put me through training in a way, giving me tools and words from Him to hold in times of pain and suffering—which I would most definitely go through later in life.

Right before this experience, I wanted to go to church and see my best friend play piano at his recital. So, I changed my clothes and went. With a PICC in my arm and looking really rough, I showed up at church. Midway through walking down the hall, I realized this might not be the best idea I've ever had. But too late to turn back now. I snuck into the back of the room and sat down. My best friend was next up, but other things were on their way up too. I noticed a small trash bin and thought, "Maybe this will work." But no guys, I was going to need a bigger boat. I stood up and went to leave when my arm was grabbed. I turned, and it was my pastor. He asked me if I was feeling alright, and I told him I wasn't. So, of course, like any good pastor, he started to pray for me. When he ended, I felt the need to throw up so strongly that I ran out the door and to the nearest toilet. When I arrived, I threw up a ton of pink mucus! I found that super odd. Later, I learned that a sign of pneumonia is a pink hue in your mucus secretion. God was cleaning me out. I raced back to the recital like a scene in a movie and busted through the back doors just in time to see him take his bow. It was tragic. However, I did feel a whole lot better after my pastor prayed, and I puked out the pneumonia. I only had a few more days of IV meds, then I was tube-free! Once I got through the most difficult battle of my life—thus far—my life was about to change for the better.

The Girl with the Face

My life soon included a new opportunity for performing: a festival of the arts between churches of the same denomination, where you compete and sharpen your ministry gifts at both a district and national level. Sounds like a little church gathering, right? *Wrong!* We are talking thousands of competing teens from sixth to twelfth grade in every category you can imagine under the umbrella of the word "Arts." I became involved with this because a friend of mine said their human video team needed an extra person. What in the world is a human video? It is one of the most creative forms of storytelling I have ever known. You tell your story using only track. Music, voice-over, and sound effects can be used, then the actors lip-sync the words and mime the story with their body only, no props. If you are confused, you can look up my YouTube account.[1] I was totally drafted into this because they needed an extra body. I had no experience and no idea what it was. The teams were put together based on talent and grade. Although I was a high school dropout, I was eighteen, and so I was the inexperienced chick that was on a team with seasoned students who had been doing this since they were in sixth grade. I was way behind the game, but I joined the team and even got to play a lead role—Satan. Nice, right? No pressure.

After the hype and excitement of us moving past the district level to the national level of the competition, I was pretty hooked. Now, human video is very much a physical art, and with less-than-perfect lungs, my doctors were not supporting this new-found love of mine. They cautioned me to be careful to not overdo it, not get in people's faces, and not break any of my fragile bones. Oh, now would be a great time to remind you that no one at my church except my pastors knew I had Cystic Fibrosis. I wasn't hospitalized enough to have people ask what was wrong, nor did I seem ill—probably because I was a pro at holding back coughs so they wouldn't be so violent. So, since I was coming into this new activity as a normal teenager, I was treated as if I had no limitations. That was how I liked it.

The time had come for signups for the 2009 festival, and I was top of the list! I was placed on the top team from my church under the dreaded coaching of Derek. This guy was hardcore and pushed us to our max. In practices, I would fall short at times, which might be why he gave me a lead part because I couldn't really hang with the group. I had good facial expressions and body language. I also did a human video small (which is less people in the group), a drama small, a drama large, and a drama solo. Yes, that's a whole lot of categories. When we got to our district competition, I would stay with my parents in a hotel room and do all my medications in secret, and everything that came with CF was kept hidden as well. I never remember being tired or out of breath while competing, which I know was God's gift to me.

After several days and rounds of competition, it was time for the celebration service. This is when they announce the winners and some of them get to perform on stage in front of all the churches in the PEN FL (Pensacola, Florida) district. Thousands are there, so it's a big deal. The most incredible

---

1   https://www.youtube.com/itsbethanybryan

thing happened. I got first place in drama solo, first place in drama small, second place in drama large, first place in human video small and in human video large . . . FIRST PLACE! It was unreal! With each placing, a medal was put around my neck. After four, I asked my mother to put them in her purse, because I was embarrassed to wear them all. I was able to perform three of my winning pieces on the stage. I was overwhelmed, as was my family and my church! My mother remembers the moment being so overwhelming that she felt as though she was literally floating off the ground. She remembers God telling her that as she released me to minister, He would heal me.

When I was leaving the celebration service, I was swarmed with people from other churches telling me how awesome I was and asking to take pictures with me. For a girl with some insecurities because of my education level and my health battles, this was a new identity . . . a winner! I wasn't used to that. I had felt like a failure before. Of course, you're always being told by your family that you are a winner, but this was life-changing for me. I was bombarded with friend requests and even a fan page someone had made. In the small drama called *Whatis-zit?* I had several scenes where I would cross my eyes. This earned me the name, "The Girl with the Face." When we went to national competition, I felt like a celebrity! It was so amazing to see people want to talk to you and take a picture with you. Some "fans" became friends that I still have today.

At the National level, my large human video, *Who's the Master?*, placed second. My small human video, *Becoming Paul*, placed second. My small drama, *Whatis-zit?*, placed sixth. As for my solo drama, let's just say it ended up being a very sad ordeal; I ended up being disqualified because my voice went out during my performance. After we came home, I uploaded the videos of the performances on my YouTube account: bethanyluvsjesus. As soon as they were posted, they took off! *Who's the Master?* was redone by churches from all over the USA but also in the Philippines, Brazil, and more. Other human videos of mine have been done in India where they contacted me asking for the music, saying even though they cannot understand the words, they can feel the anointing. So incredible. In 2010, I continued to do the college-age competition called Kappa Tau where my groups placed first in small human video and small drama. I also placed first in solo human video and solo drama through Kappa Tau the following year. I never broke a bone. Shortness of breath never kept me from performing. God truly blessed me to do what I loved.

Arts Festival was a form of worship for me. It was a way of giving my talents to God and pushing past the physical limitations that the doctors told me I had. I did it because of my passion to show the message of God's love. It remains a part of my life to this day. I have been coaching since 2012. My husband came right alongside me and fell in love with this art as well. He is a phenomenal human video coach, and together, we have created some amazing stories and performances. Through coaching, he and I have had the opportunity to mentor close to 100+ teenagers and teach them about passion and challenge them to go deeper in their relationship with Jesus. I'm so thankful for what Arts Festival did for me and what it allows me to do for others. Around this time, when I was riding the wave of success, boys began to come out of nowhere.

I do not want to go into great detail about my "love life" because I do not want to make this a romance novel. I'm totally kidding! There isn't enough content to be anything more than a sappy car commercial. However, part of my story is how God brought me the perfect person to be my husband. As a teen, I naturally had crushes, but my first real crush was also my best friend. It was a friendship with a strong foundation, but I kept my illness from him, just like I did from everyone else. After our relationship never seemed to move past the friendship level even though I really wanted it to, we began to drift apart. The change made me begin to think my secret was out and it would do exactly what I feared it would—dictate my life. This was a confirmation to me that keeping it hidden was the right route. I couldn't tell anyone. Not yet. I wasn't ready to be treated as fragile by everyone or have every greeting be, "How are you feeling?" I liked being healthy to them.

Another one of my friends started showing signs of wanting more than a friendship with me. He and I were in several Arts Festival entries together, so we spent a lot of time together. We both became "Arts Festival legends" (as they called us), so it was almost expected that we should date, and that was why our friendship became something more. I kept my illness from him as well, and he was my first official boyfriend. We were Facebook official, so it was legit. We were young. I prayed at the start of that relationship that if it wasn't God's plan, God would have it end slowly. Not some heart-shattering breakup leaving nothing behind, not even a friendship. I wanted to stay friends, because that's why we fell in love to begin with. After my first kiss was given to him, the breakup began . . . slowly, just like I asked. We began sitting apart at church, but still hugging and saying hello. It was like all feelings were going away, and we didn't know why. When he finally decided there was nothing left to hold on to, he broke up with me. He explained that he didn't know why his feelings had changed, because he still wanted to love me. I knew why. We were not meant to be more than friends, and the great part is, we still are friends. Today, his wife and I are such encouragements to each other through the physical battles we both face.

I never was one to pursue relationships because I was okay being single. My parents gave me so much positive affirmation that I wasn't starving for attention. I remained single for a year, and then there came . . . Jack. (You will hear more about him later!) In the year I was alone, I went through a lot of growing spiritually. I had a revelation that I was *healed* regardless of the doctors not seeing it. This happened after having an awesome appointment where my PFT (pulmonary function test) numbers were really, really great. I remember how I felt as I watched the computer screen show what I was striving so hard for. Blasting every last bit of air out until I had nothing left. The office was full of praise and also reality being spoken all at once. I was one happy girl. I asked one of the pastors if I could give my testimony on a Wednesday night. He agreed and scheduled it right away. I didn't tell anyone what I was going to be speaking about, but the curiosity grew and grew. The night came, and the room was packed! People were standing. My family and even distant family members came. My childhood friends came to support me. I was told my senior pastor even snuck in to hear me.

As the pastor called me up to the mic, I took a moment and looked at all the faces. I was about to tell everyone the secret I had kept hidden so I wouldn't be treated different. This could change everything. But I told them all about Cystic Fibrosis and some of my story. I was honest and vulnerable. I did it because I wanted to share my testimony. I was claiming my healing. I described it as a child at the store whose parent just bought them something they had been asking for. If the parent paid for it and is handing it to them, the child wouldn't keep asking for it because it's theirs. They would grab it and own it and thank them for it! That's what I felt I should do regarding my healing. Take it, claim it as mine, and tell everyone what God had already done and just keep thanking Him for it. The room was so quiet, no one being distracted, and it was as if everyone looked at me with new eyes. I knew my life would be different from here on, but I also felt free. No more being ashamed of being different. Instead, being proud I was alive. (Side Note: A new perspective will change your life. Don't look at your story through a filter of bitterness, but rather through a filter of thankfulness.) My best friend (the one who things never moved past friendship with) came to the altar and hugged me and cried, and he told me how much he loved me, which meant so much. My ex-boyfriend came up and hugged me, and I told him I was sorry for not being honest with him. He told me it wouldn't have changed anything.

Then a boy I didn't know came to the altar. I had noticed him several times throughout the night, so I was definitely wanting to pray with him. I walked to him, and one of my friends introduced him as Beau, who was born with CF. Without hesitation and even to his surprise, I pulled him in for a hug. I held him close, and I prayed for him long and hard. That was the first time either of us hugged another CF patient like that. Cystic Fibrosis patients are not supposed to get any closer than six feet to each other due to the risk of cross-infection, which is basically catching one another's infections/bugs. Even though the risk was high, Beau and I quickly became very close, closer than six feet. This was the first time in my life that, when a friend said, "I understand what you are going through," he really did. We both were great at acting. So, I recruited him for Arts Festival!

We both competed in a human video and small drama together. Practices were held at my house, where we would often be found eating Cajun chicken strips and watching cartoons through the night. He was like a brother to me, and my sister and my parents also basically adopted him. I know God had His hand of protection on him and me. It was as if we were immune to each other's bugs. I still talk to him every once in a while, and we always make a point to see each other when we can. No worries about getting each other sick. A gift from God.

After my "revealing," things did change for me. No one could have a conversation without asking me how I was feeling. They treated me as if I was fragile, but it didn't seem to bother the guys. I still had a few try to date me, and one not interested whatsoever. Cue, Jack.

Potato Night

The first time I spoke to Jack was on behalf of a friend. She wanted to know the name of the one she called "college boy." Our church had separate departments for youth and young adults. I and everyone in my life were in the youth group, while Jack was in the young adults. It wasn't love at first sight for either of us. In fact, he will tell you he thought I was cross-eyed. I thought he was loaded, because the man knew how to dress. I walked over to get his name for my friend like this: "Hi, that girl likes you. What's your name?" It was subtle, charming, and I'm sure top ten first impression worthy. This began the acquaintance where we would talk to one another about our boyfriend and girlfriend. He would tell me to break up with mine, because he was not for me. I would tell him his girlfriend was lying, and she actually was wearing makeup in that selfie she sent him. Just playfully picking on each other's relationships. It was nothing to write in my diary about. He was just . . . Jack.

Eventually, I noticed him at the sound board with my father a lot, and my mother would talk his ears off, probably telling him my whole life story like she normally would to everyone. I love her so much. (Side Note: My mother has a gift of always turning any subject into a conversation about God. As a child I didn't appreciate this, but now I am amazed by the number of people she has shared Jesus with.) She was a big fan of his, and to this day, she is convinced the sparks started at a baked potato dinner the worship arts department had. My mother sat at the table with him and his sister. She made a point to call me over and tell me that his sister was truly his sister, not his girlfriend, which I guess is what she thought. (Fun Fact: My mother buys him Mr. Potato Head shirts when she can, because of this moment.)

Fast forward awhile—I had been single for about a year. My mother ran into my room with my phone. She was using it to look at my Facebook because she didn't want to get one herself, but she did want to keep up with everyone. This happened often, and I would always be surprised when all the pages she "liked" began to post to my wall. She came bursting into my room saying, "Jack just changed his relationship status to 'single.' Message him!" I didn't argue because, why not? I'll just casually ask him what happened to his relationship that we used to talk about. I texted him and he explained that he had been single for awhile but was just getting around to making it public. I was a good friend and acted like I cared. "Man, I'm sorry to hear that," I said as my mother and I smiled at each other. Oh yes, this was about to happen.

I started texting him more and more, and for the first time ever, I was the one making all the moves. This was extremely out of the norm for me, since I was taught to let the guy pursue me. But I just felt like I had to get him before someone else did. He had such high standards; he was a virgin, and he even wanted to wait until his wedding day to kiss. You don't find guys like that. Eventually, he fell for me like they all do. (That's a joke.) But it took a little time. He did the respectful thing and asked my father for permission to date me. As a family, we took him to a restaurant; the very reason for this was for him to ask my father for permission, so it was elegant at the table. I was excited and a little nervous, but I knew how much my father approved of him, so after plenty of jokes (and I'm sure a few playful hidden threats for Jack to pick up on), I excused myself to the bathroom in hopes it would happen in private. But when I came back with my sister to the table, my father right away said, "Well, are you going to ask me or what?" I just had to go with it, so I placed my elbows on the table and held my face up in my hands real close to him. I looked into his perfect face, batting my eyes in an attempt to be irresistibly too cute to allow his nerves to keep him from asking. I can't forget his surprised look at how sudden the question came, giving him no preparation time. That was my father's strategy, I'm sure—make him comfortable with small talk and stories, then, BAM, pressure. Jack handled it as well as he could. I could almost hear his heart beating, yet his voice remained strong as he asked my father for permission to date his daughter. It was a special moment. After we became official, like possibly the very same day, I felt it was time to tell him I loved him. So, I did it through a text, and I wasn't even nervous about it. I just waited for him to respond. It took awhile, which was a little confusing to me because he should definitely love me already. Right? He finally responded, "I can't say that right now." Love was more than just a word to him. I admired that after the fact, but it felt really awkward in that exact moment. I told myself, "No big deal, just brush it off. He'll come around."

The first time we were somewhat alone was on a Wednesday night before a church service. Because my father worked at the church, you could often find me there hours before church time. There was a small love seat and TV in the youth building, so I brought a cute movie and decided to make a date of it. It was sort of like a date at home in the living room, just with the occasional interruption of my youth pastor checking on us. As soon as we were alone, I began to bring my face really close to his, knowing I was crossing some personal boundaries, but I was sneaky like that. I started cuddling his face with mine, and in a total of about three seconds, I made my way to his lips and BOOM, sneak attacked him! I kissed him very quickly so he couldn't pull away or tell me no. I expected him to be shocked at first, but then, like every movie I'd seen where they did the sneak attack, he would look into her eyes as if she just placed him under her enchantment, grab her face and pull her in for a nice big one! That's not what happened. He looked at me shocked, and then he said nothing and did nothing. So, we just watched the movie in silence. Again, much like the "I love you" tragedy, I went home and regretted my straightforwardness. At least I was banking on the fact that he may *have* to marry me now.

Despite our awkward start, our relationship was beautiful, and we were both very happy. After we had been together for several months, we came up with a system where we would ask what percent we were at regarding marriage. This was how we told each other how sure we were that we were meant to be. We always stayed around 50%. That was until a church event one night when the Spirit of God was moving, and Jack prayed over me, asking God for a confirmation that we were for each other. As he was praying,

God told him, "She's a yes." He didn't tell me right then because he wanted God to tell me.

We continued our relationship, and eventually his family invited me to go with them to a revival service in Cleveland, Tennessee. I was looking forward to being with his family. In the first hotel we stayed at, his sister and I were in a room together which was attached to the room Jack and his parents were in. We must have gone to four or five services in one weekend. They were used to services like that, lasting hours and hours, then running to grab a quick fast-food meal before rushing back to another long service. It took some getting used to for me, and I'm still not going to tell you I handle them as well as they do. Especially when my tummy starts growling. However, I have learned to respect the anointing, and I love being in it and letting God move through the minister without looking at the time.

The rich anointing Jack grew up in and around was so attractive to me. I wanted nothing more than to marry a man who loved Jesus more than anything, and that was Jack. I was falling so deeply in love with him that it was beginning to hurt to think that God had not confirmed to me that I would marry him. So, in a service, I prayed, begging God over and over to tell me right then if Jack was my husband. It was during the offering when He did. I heard clear as day, audible in almost a sarcastic tone, an "Okay" followed by my name with Jack's last name. I even looked behind me to see if someone was messing with me. But it was God! I smiled at Jack, and anxiously waited for three hours for the service to end so I could tell him I was finally at 100%! The service ended, and we got into the car. To my surprise, he texted me asking, "What percent are you?" I grinned as I typed 100% and pressed send. He smiled from ear to ear and replied, "Me too!" Thank God for seatbelts, because we would have been floating otherwise. I found out that Jack also had a moment when he heard from God. God told him to put all of the money in his wallet in the offering. He had quite a bit, since he was on a trip with his girlfriend. When he placed the money into the bucket, God told him, "You just bought your answer." I don't often try to figure God out because I never want to be wrong and make a mess of things, but I can't help but think Jack's obedience had something to do with me hearing my confirmation. I know Jack had been asking God to speak to me about being married; remember, he already had his confirmation. My confirmation bought with his obedience. Incredible, right?

On what was now the best trip of my life, where I was making such a great impression on his family, fear had to show up and try to mess up everything. I had been doing well up to this point. Jack had become my security, and I felt safe when I was beside him. The whole trip we had adjoining rooms, so he was right there if I needed anything. At the hotel where we stayed on one of the last days, his father had to book a room for me and Jack's sister a few doors down from Jack and his parent's room. I began to feel out of breath as Jack walked me to my room to say goodnight. It felt so far away from him, too far for comfort. I didn't really know his sister well at this point, and Jack was my security. We got to the door, and my heart was going at a rate I'm sure he could hear. Things got worse as I noticed the door to the room beside ours was open. I leaned over to see in, and I thought I saw a dead body under the bed, but Jack assured me there was nothing, trying to calm me down. At that moment, the door slammed, and I began shaking and crying and told Jack I couldn't stay and that I needed him to not leave me. Going from calm to absolutely terrified must have been alarming to Jack, but he walked me back to his parents, and what happened next was the most embarrassing display of my battle with fear yet.

I began to swing at Jack and scratch him all down his face, hurting the best thing that had ever happened to me. The one I loved, and who God had just confirmed I was to spend my life with. I remember his father saying, "Hold her son. Pray over her!" Jack scooped me up like a child and laid me on his chest and just prayed as he held me. I remember them all praying over me and speaking scriptures. My next memory is waking up next to his mother and getting up to go to the bathroom. She came a few seconds later to the bathroom door and asked me if I was okay. I said, "Yes ma'am." In that bathroom, trying to get my thoughts together and feeling so many emotions, I tried my hardest to cry silently so they wouldn't hear me. The embarrassment I felt was crippling. I blew it, and I was certain Jack's family would tell him to run as far away from me as he could, and I could expect nothing else. The next morning, I was quiet and awkward. I just wanted to go home.

At some point, when I became bold enough to address it, I broke down and told him how sorry I was and how I wouldn't expect him to stay with me after seeing that. He looked very shocked and told me all I did was curl up in the hotel chair in the corner and cry as he came over and held me and they all prayed. I couldn't believe it. Very much like the experience I had lying on my living room couch, feeling and living physically what was going on spiritually. Again, no physical proof of my "reality." Jack had no marks on his face, just like I had no damage to the back of my head. I was so glad that what I had experienced was only for me to go through. I really thought I would lose Jack because of this. It's hard to explain this, but much like the experience on the couch at my parents' house, I go through these intense fear moments where there are no signs of the attack I live out. I know that is because these moments, which are very few and far between, are spiritual, and I live them out in the moment.

Soon, Jack asked for permission to marry me. His proposal was beautiful, thoughtful, and perfect. But soon after that, my world shifted. Tragedy hit my home. My father lost his job due to a conditional cycle that my mother and I were all too familiar with. We prayed against it often and feared its return.

A Family Secret

When I was younger, maybe around six or seven, I remember my father acting strange, distant, and not himself. He would gaze out into nothing with very glassy-looking eyes and just sit there until he was spoken to, then he would try to search his mind for the proper reaction to what was said. He was detached from his surroundings, but he was never violent, and he never made me feel like he was going to hurt me. I knew it was my father who loved me with all his heart, but I also knew that this was a stranger. I remember hugging him and him smiling at me but pulling me gently off of him, as you would do to a stranger who was making you feel uncomfortable. This hurt me. I can remember how I felt as his glazed eyes looked into my hurt face. This was my first time meeting this version of my father, but it was far from my last.

I couldn't tell you how many times we walked through these mental breakdowns, but I can tell you they would have a familiar cycle which would help my mother and I "prepare" for them the best way we could, but also try to prevent them. He desired to be the very best provider for our family of four, which often meant multiple jobs and long hours. He wanted my mother to stay home if she could, but when she would get a job, it was usually at the place I went to school so she could be close to me and my sister.

My father struggled to remain faithful to his marriage vows and battled with pornography, which led to infidelity. I remember being old enough to understand what this meant and how it hurt my mother, and it hurt me at a young age. His addiction would appear and lead to overwhelming guilt and fear, which led to more stress than just the working-long-hours stress, which would lead to a breakdown. It all seemed to flow in this way. It was considered a cycle, and my mother and I always knew one was coming from the look his eyes would get. Then he would come home, always chewing lots of gum nonstop, and she would begin to ask him if he was dipping chewing tobacco again, which he would take up when he was stressed. After several times around the cycle, and in the hope of finding freedom, he agreed to go stay at a ministry center in Kentucky, which was like a Bible boot camp. I believe there was no contact allowed with anyone outside, besides weekend visits. Only men lived there, and they worked and had church and Bible studies every day.

At the time, I was around nine and a half and my sister was almost one and a half. My mother, sister, and I were staying with friends and family for a while until she decided she wanted to go be near him. We were connected to a sweet family's home only a few miles away from where my father was. This family would open up their doors, often for young teenage girls who needed help at a desperate point in their lives. Only one other mother was there with her few children; the rest were teenagers. As you can imagine, my little fat-cheeked sister was the center of all their attention, as I was usually outside singing to the goats and playing with the endless number of kittens that kept multiplying. They also gave me plenty of attention, and I have a photo of me dancing for them. I have so many memories during the six months we lived there—like making mud pies and eating the strongest pot of French onion soup I ever had in my life. We had to all go outside as it cooked because we couldn't see through the tears. God really blessed us with this new family of strangers who we became so attached to and loved.

Visiting Daddy was rare and strange, and it was sad to see all the fathers who didn't have their children close enough to visit often. A few of them would spoil Tearsa and me with little gifts they all would get from the Gibson factories they worked at. So much stationery! I wrote notes to everyone with them. The hardest part was leaving at the end of the day. I understood the situation, but Tearsa didn't, and it was hard on her. Each visit was the same thing. It never got easier saying goodbye, and I would always count how much longer we had to visit as soon as we arrived. One time, for only a few hours, they let him go eat with us. It felt strange to have him out and be just us as a family again. We got through the whole experience and made some incredible connections for life. I am still connected through Facebook with the lovely family we lived with there.

We later moved to Washington State, where my father's family lived. It was a very different environment than we were used to. We went from Florida, where we had not only my mother's enormous family—who were full of faith—but all our church friends, too, to Washington, where we had the opposite. Few on my father's side were Christians, and we settled into a comfortable Baptist church that was entirely new to us Pentecostal folk. Soon, my father was leading us right into another cycle as he fell back into his addictions, and this time, I found him out. His sins always caught up to him no matter how good he got at hiding them. His entire personality would begin to become the evidence of his unfaithfulness. He would come clean if asked by my mother. She said she always knew when he was struggling. This particular time, someone called the house phone and I answered. The person on the other end spoke in a calm and cunning manner. They gave me a name to tell my father and told me to "be sure and tell him I called." Then they made a point to tell me they liked a poster we had in the hallway, naming the band it was of, which was their way of letting me know they had been in the house. I felt like a parent catching their child in a lie. I would like to think I would have told my mother right away, and then even reprimanded my father, venting all my feelings of being disappointed (again) and how exposed I felt knowing some stranger knew my home now and felt the need to describe the poster to me which now has planted yet another seed of fear on top of the one growing because I am now in fear that you are heading toward another breakdown! Layers upon layers of fear, distrust, and feeling unsafe.

A few days went by, and we noticed a white car had been pulling up to our house and just sitting there while my father was gone. We all felt unsafe, to say the least. We held it together for a quick holiday visit from my brother, Chris, who we had not seen in far too long. It was his first time meeting Tearsa, and things were far from perfect in his world, but having him back was nice, and he was so great at jumping right into the brother role even after being away so long. He showed how much he truly cared about my health by always going above and beyond to keep his smoking addiction as far from me as he could, washing up and smoking outside and letting his clothes air out. I remember all he would do for my sake, and it really meant a lot. I always hated to see him leave, and I know if he would have ever decided to live with or near us, we would have had the very best of memories more often. But even with distance and time against us, anytime he would come back, it was like he never left, and our time was super-special and cherished. After Chris had left us, we soon noticed my father began to get quiet, and my mother couldn't hide her fear from me, even if she wanted to. At this point, I was completely in this with her and beside her. Being so far away from her family and support system, we became closer, and I would try to help carry the load with her even though she would never ask that of her child. I was the protector when my father was weak. I took that mantle, and I can remember many times taking on a much bigger role than I needed to and should have. This wasn't my mother's fault, nor my father's; it was who I was. I wanted to fix things, hold things together, and protect each member of my family through the hard times. When you walk through hard times, like we often did, not only do you learn a system to make it through, but it's like another level of closeness is birthed. Hard times bring you to a place of deeper connection, communication, and relationship with each other.

My mother and I were certain we were about to go through the very worst part of his cycle, so we prepared this time. We packed up the house and contacted a couple who helped my father as a young man and new baby Christian. They were the only thing close to a Christian, safe environment my mother could think of. Glory Mountain was where they lived, a beautiful, huge home tucked back on the top of the high mountains of Washington State. They had a small home attached to their garage, and that is where we lived. My father was unable to work right away, but wasn't completely gone this time. It was like we caught it before it fully happened.

Tearsa and I began having some mountain adventures and ate many blackberries, raspberries, and orange salmonberries. (Fun Fact: I loved to come up with ideas to put some extra cash in our pockets. Food was always my main concern. These orange salmonberries were quite rare, and I was ready to make all kinds of jellies with the over-abundance we had on the side of the mountain. One day, I was explaining my ideas to the owner of the mountain home, and he told me those berries just appeared one day; he had never seen them before. He then told me they came from the poop of birds which must have ate them and brought them over to his part of the mountain. He talked like it was a good thing. I remember being devastated that I had been eating my weight in poop berries for weeks now. There went my hopes of being rich.) Tearsa and I were both enrolled in a somewhat small private school where mother got a job working in the daycare. Eighth grade was a tough grade to be thrown into all of a sudden, because I had been homeschooled since third grade. I learned much about the world and myself in the brief time I was there. I learned I was insecure in many ways and even angry inside, and this is where it began to surface due to peer pressure to fit in no matter what. I even found bullying as a way to cope. It didn't matter if you were sweet to me or if I called you my best friend. I am very sad to admit it, but I would even mildly make fun of those with disabilities because I was bitter that I was born with some myself. I struggled to learn and was quick to give up if I couldn't understand. Usually, I would just pretend that I understood and figure out a way to cheat. I would mask my failures with jokes or a tough exterior, and it didn't help at all that I always seemed to like the "bad boys" because I was drawn to the confidence and moxie they would so boldly exude. I was a follower through and through at this age.

We lived on the mountain until my father was well enough to get a job and get us all back to our normal. From there, we went to a creepy old house in a small town with a nightmare of a public school—uprooted yet again and thrown into a new chapter, hoping this one would have a happy ending that would last. I was enrolled at the school, which was within walking distance, and there began my first experience with the real world without a Christian filter. Coming from a school where I was a bully, I instantly became a target for bullying. My father bought me PE sweats that were three times my size so no boys would be checking me out, and my mother paid for me to get double portions during lunch to keep me gaining weight, and I was bold about being a Christian because I had no idea how much of a target you become when you advertise something like that. I was thrashed. I was cussed out by kids in my face and made fun of for being so sickly. It was a harsh, rude awakening. I began to ask my parents to take me out, and once I even skipped school and just sat in the woods. I was pulled out and went back to homeschooling, and I could breathe again. Back home to safety. Me, my mother, and my little Tearsa Joy.

We truly were the best of friends, and we enjoyed using our imaginations daily. Our education was lacking due to the absence of consistency, but we would always make the best of things. Eighth grade was my last time at a regular school; for my sister it was second grade. There were times our mother would try to make learning a game for us, and we watched plenty of educational shows, but it was hard to want to do schoolwork. Homeschooling curriculum was expensive, and we really couldn't afford it. Even with missing out on such an important part of schooling and growing up, it never felt as though we were lacking or missing out in any way. I always remember being happy in the midst of the instability, and boy do we have the very best of stories.

We moved again because my mother kept getting really sick since we moved into the house. Black mold grew on the walls, and the house was unlivable for us, especially with CF in the picture. By God's grace, I never got sick while we lived there.

After several years in Washington, we decided it was time to take a road trip to visit my mother's family in Florida. The trip went great, but on the way home, we stopped in Texas to see my brother, Chris, and his wife. We ended up spending more than we should have, resulting in us making it to California and running out of money, then gas. We were sitting at the gas station, melting because it was so hot. Tearsa, who was around six at this time, was crying in her car seat, and I could feel hopelessness fill the car. My father was fine one moment, then he started staring with that look. My mother and I made eye contact, as if to say, "Please God, no." This was not the ideal place for this—no one to help us, no idea where to go, and no way to shelter Tearsa from it, who was now old enough to be confused and fearful of this other version of her father—a version she had never met. I watched as my father, sitting in the driver's seat, slowly turned and looked at my mother's worried face, and said, "I don't know what to do."

She and I handled things as best as we could, while of course praying nonstop. We were switching into survival mode. We made him move to the passenger's side and I sat behind him. My mother left the car for a moment and made a phone call to her family, and they wired us the money to fill up the car and settle into a hotel for the night. Her brother was given a dream that night of his father (who had passed years ago) telling him to get on a plane and come to California to drive us back to Florida. As my mother drove to the hotel, she was trying to hide the panic in her voice and remain calm enough to drive the highways of California for the first time—hard enough for a skilled driver, but she hardly ever drove because we almost always had only one vehicle, which my father used for work. As we were nearing our exit, without warning, my father almost calmly took off his seat belt, opened his door, and put his leg nearly halfway out. The car erupted with panic as my mother yelled the name of Jesus in prayer, Tearsa cried, and I, without hesitation, instantly took off my belt and reached my small, bony arms around my father, holding him in the seat and praying as my heart pounded. It felt like slow motion as I was both afraid but strong, with my face pressed against the back of his seat. He looked over at my mother, and with tears in his eyes, he said something like, "I have to die, so you don't have to." She told him that was not true and talked him into closing his door. I finally was able to exhale; it felt like I was holding my breath the whole time. We went through many more hard things with him on that trip, but God's hand was on us the whole time. (Author's Addition: Thinking back on this moment brings me so much emotion. It was a sacrifice he was talking about here. He understood, even in his confused mind, that his actions were hurting us. I know the enemy was lying to him, saying he should do this to protect us. My father loves his family; this was an example of that. The enemy knows you, and he has studied what you care about. He does his homework. If he didn't, his strategies would not be so specific. He is the father of lies, yet he also twists the truth and has been doing it for years. You have to filter your thoughts and do what the Bible says in 2 Corinthians 10:5, which talks about taking your thoughts captive. It's really simple to know who your thoughts are from and whose agenda it is. To steal, kill, and destroy is the devil's agenda. Jeremiah 29:11 is God's agenda, and it's the exact opposite of the devil's. You see how the devil exploited my father's sacrificial love for us and used that special, God-implanted characteristic to try to kill him. The devil is tricky. Don't fall for his manipulation. He can appear as an angel of light, but he isn't. He's a counterfeit of light, and I really hate him. But, spoiler alert, he straight up loses in the end man!)

We were brought back to Florida, and when my father returned to us mentally (these breakdowns usually lasted from a few weeks to a month or so), he said God had told him to stay in Florida, but he had gone back to Washington because he had a great job waiting. Not that God caused this, but He used the cycle to bring us where we needed to be. It would have been a lot less dramatic if my father would have just listened, but you can't win them all! The transition back to living in Florida wasn't smooth by any means; it took us a while to get on our feet, and we lived with multiple family members for about a year and a half. We were not able to get our belongings back from Washington and lost contact with our friends who packed up our entire house for us and said they would hold onto our memories at least. That's all my mother asked them to keep. Losing all our belongings except for what fit in a small luggage carrier affected my mother more than any of us. That was our whole lives: wedding stuff, baby stuff, anything and every-thing we had . . . gone. This loss caused her to save nearly everything. She was always seen carrying multiple bags with her, I think in fear of ending up with only what she could carry, but she was also saving all our drawings and things to make sure we had memories and things we could look back on. Tearsa remembers very little of that trip back from California; we tried to make things seem as normal as possible for her as we went through it, and God was there. But the next time this would happen, she would be right in the middle of it.

Now we are back to when I had just got engaged to Jack. Thankfully, my father was able to give his approval right before another breakdown hit. He went to work one morning normal, then came home in a full-blown episode. We had no clue how he was even able to drive himself home. He lost his job because he couldn't work, making my part-time job the only income. Jack would take me to the landlord's house so I could pay the rent, which was $600 short of what it should have been, but thank God, our landlords were great people and they allowed us to live there on whatever I could pay. Jack would also bring food to last us for the week and drive me where I needed to go. This was such an embarrassing way to begin life with my future husband, but he never made me feel anything less than adored, and he was very com-forting to have during the cycle this time.

The hard part was watching my sister go through this for the first time. She was much older than I was when I first went through it. We had to tell her of the past times, which made her feel left out of this family secret. Of course, we had prayed and hoped that each time would be the last, so it was something we hoped she would never have to deal with. This was a lot on her and a lot on me. I regretted my engagement to Jack only because now he was involved in this and was carrying part of the load. We had already set a wedding date. I knew how long it took to get my father back on his feet. How could I get married and leave my family with no income? I just couldn't. With so many boxes already checked off, we decided to continue with the wedding as planned and trust that God would work everything out. I wasn't happy about it; in fact, I was crushed and scared at the thought of it. But Jack kept telling me it would all be okay, and the thought of being his wife kept me in high spirits.

One day, very, very shortly before the wedding, my father walked into my room and sat on my bed, and we had a heart-to-heart. I basically remember telling him how I was leaving, and how desperately I wanted the family to never go through this again without me being there to help play the part I always had the times before—mother's shoulder to cry on and prayer partner, my sister's distraction, and my father's comfort. This last time with him, I sat beside him and prayed over his mind to be at peace, speaking scriptures over him. I didn't want to leave him like this.

Then God showed up. Right before the wedding day, he looked at me and asked, "Did I miss your wedding?" It was a moment I will never forget. He recovered the fastest he ever had. It was God's gift to me. Now, I could be excited to marry my Jack!

New Name, New Life

NEW NAME, NEW LIFE

Jack and I are entertainers. He is a musician, and I am an aspiring actress who never has time to pursue any auditions. So, I'm kind of just waiting for a big producer to knock on my door. Because of who we are, we were open to not having a traditional church wedding. Even though God is the absolute center of both of our lives, He is not confined to a church building, so we were set on bringing God into our wedding despite the missing pulpit and pews. We were married in the historic Florida Theater. Jack got dressed in the room Elvis Presley did, and the stage that hosts *The Nutcracker* each holiday season was the one on which we would become hitched for life. How in the world did we afford this dream wedding when my small check from Cracker Barrel was paying my family's rent? This is a perfect example of God's provision, and it was also further confirmation that we were supposed to be together, and the timing was God's.

The venue was paid for by Jack's family, and we even were blessed with a discounted price. The flowers were covered by my grandmother on my father's side. Our reception food was catered by my mother's family. All my decorations were paid for by my aunt on my father's side. Our friends said they would be our photographers—for free. A tremendously busy friend of mine who owned a production company offered to do our video for free because I did some projects with him for no pay. My makeup and hair were done for free. My coordinator did everything because she loved us, asking for nothing in return. When I tell you this wedding was my dream, I mean it. Jack and I paid for our cake. The lady took off half the price after meeting us because she fell in love with who we were. We also paid for my wedding dress, which I had circled in a magazine two years earlier. I brought the magazine to the store two weeks before my wedding date, and they told me it had been discontinued for a while, but they would check in the back. Guess what? They came out with one, and you guessed it, it was exactly my size. All the way down to our getaway car and our hotel room for the night . . . all of it was taken care of. Unbelievable.

On the day of my wedding, my parents woke me up and took me out to eat. We enjoyed our time together, and there were some tears but mostly excitement. We arrived at the venue, and Jack, who had been there for hours already, was a good distance away on the opposite side of the theater so he wouldn't see me. My grandma had all the beautiful bouquets laid out on the bar, and the first thing she said to me was, "I sure hope you ate your Wheaties this morning, girl. This thing is heavy." She wasn't kidding; the bouquet was over a dozen roses jam-packed with calla lilies in the center. I made my way up to get ready and snacked on some Chick-fil-A nuggets from the snack bar that someone made for me and all my girls. No idea who did that, but thank you if you are reading this. I was so relaxed and not stressed that I even forgot my shoes. The doors were about to open, and I had my father's arm. We were smiling and laughing together. Suddenly, I thought to myself, "I have a foot itch, let me just rub it on this carpet . . . wait, where are my shoes?" Thankfully, my lovely friend Kelli ran up several flights of stairs to the dressing room then back down and slipped them onto my feet, seconds before the doors swung open. Now that's a relaxed bride.

The wedding was beautiful. We said our vows in front of the red curtain, then it lifted to reveal a white sheet with sunset-colored clouds projected on it. Jack's father led us in communion and prayer, and my cousin, Kasey, did a beautiful ballet dance to "In Christ Alone." Then, our families did the wax beads symbolizing the families coming together. Lastly, the white sheet was lifted, and I saw, for the first time, my reception all set up: tables, cake, and lights. Everything exactly how I told my aunt I would like it. We took photos, which were all beautiful thanks to my sweet friends. Then we danced! Jack and I had a choreographed dance with multiple songs and dance styles, but we didn't account for all the fake rose petals I wanted scattered all over the stage, so I slipped around like a wet seal on a frozen lake. When it came time for the Daddy/Daughter dance, we had to make it serious. So, we did a human video. We danced a little, and of course, he made me cry as he whispered, "You're my hero."

We left that day with such peace that God was in this. My family was going to be great and provided for, and our wedding was literally blessing after blessing. It wasn't over. We rode in the car one of our groomsmen paid for to the hotel one of my aunts got us, and we opened cards, which held over $3,000 for our honeymoon. We later found out that the count for our wedding guests was a little over 900. Now, we were married. Those vows would be put to the ultimate test. For better, for worse, in sickness and in health. Till death do us part.

Not only did we have a blessed marriage, I was walking into a family that had obeyed God's Word and because of the faithfulness of Jack's parents, blessings came to us. We were able to move into a brand-new house which we built. We had a paid-off car and two full-time jobs working for the family ministry and school. Yes . . . a school. Anyone who knows me knows how I feel about school. Funny how God placed me right back into the education field along with Jack's entire family of teachers. They have conversations that I honestly zone out of because I can't comprehend their advanced vocabulary. It's been a journey of facing and overcoming some major insecurities. I couldn't help in the classrooms, even when I needed to just help a student with some work, because I wasn't able to do the work myself. His family also owned a daycare. Yes, a daycare full of kids, which meant tons of germs. But I was great at changing diapers and felt more in my element around the drooling babies rather than the intimidating high school students who kept asking me for help with their fractions. Fractions are a big *nope!*

My first clinic visit with my husband was far from pleasant. I knew that once they found out I was working at a daycare, I was going to get an ear full. We went, and as they took me out of the room to go for X-rays, my lovely doctor decided to put the fear of God in my brand-new husband. "You know your wife is dying, right?" Jack sat there, shocked at the heartless outburst, and couldn't even respond. She continued with, "She will die faster if she doesn't take her medication. Which is where you have to help. She has to take this medication to live longer." I entered the room to a very awkward stare from Jack and a grin from my doctor as if nothing happened at all. I am sure my doctor's intentions were to provide my newbie husband with a "reality check" on just how serious Cystic Fibrosis is. I can look on it now with that perspective and appreciate her straightforwardness. But at that time, I felt as though she was somehow trying to scare off my new husband. It also didn't help that my numbers were down in every way: lung function, weight, SpO (Blood Oxygen Saturation), etc. We walked out with several prescriptions.

Jack told me about his encounter with my CF doctor, which didn't make a great first impression on his super-full-of-faith-self, and he said he voiced his views on her death sentence in a short and blunt way. We talked about the medications, and I gave him some information on what they do and, most importantly, what they don't do. "They don't cure me." Then as a faith-driven, CF-knowledge-lacking husband, he asked me why I continue to take them if they fix nothing. As a youngster, I got tired of being told to take my meds anyway. Now as an adult, able to make my own choices, I started questioning too. From what I was seeing, there had been no huge improvements. So, I stopped taking them—all but my original treatments of albuterol to open my lungs up, hypertonic saline to help get rid of mucus buildup, and enzymes to help digest and absorb my food. No big-name CF drugs anymore, which is what they give you to help fight/control the infections that get trapped in the mucus buildup in the lungs. I had exactly three months before my next appointment, and I didn't do a single treatment of the medication the doctor prescribed. We came in to the appointment, did the X-ray and the pulmonary function test (PFT), and waited for the doctor to come in and discuss the results. She came in, beaming with joy, praising my numbers and the medication.

We sat there smiling, and she could tell something was up, so she asked, "What's going on?" I looked her in the face and said, "I didn't do a single treatment of the medication you prescribed. Guess my albuterol and saline are doing a great job." She had nothing to say to us, so she walked out and sent in a nurse with a flu shot. Don't get the wrong idea, not all doctors are like her. I have met some of the sweetest doctors who really care about me and don't just prescribe every medication and tell me I'm going to die if I don't take it. In the natural, that's true! Cystic Fibrosis is terminal. But remember the foundation of faith I was raised to have; death was more of an impossibility than healing for me. I wasn't going back to that doctor, so I ordered plenty of my medication that I felt worked and planned on never looking back. At least not until I needed more. But I'd figure that out later.

During this time of not pursuing normal clinic visits like I was supposed to, I ended up having food poisoning, which had me throwing up so much that I became very dehydrated. On top of that, I had a bowel obstruction causing my stomach to become visibly knotted up, bloated, and hard. Jack was the absolute best and would carry me to the bathroom, and *always*, anytime throughout our marriage, would hold my hair back as I threw up, praying out loud over me. On the bottom right side, almost in line with the top of my pelvis, there is the scar where they had to operate on me as a new-born and remove the part of my intestines that had become blocked and crystallized. Very often, after a large meal, I would hurt there; it was as if the scar tissue or something made it hard to pass that turn during the digestion process. Jack would literally massage that area for me to help it go through. It really did help me so much, but this time, I was in such excruciating pain, I asked him to call my mother to come be with us. Now I had both of my rocks beside me. I was crying so hard and asking my mother to sing the heal-ing song she always had when I was growing up. It's called "I Am The God That Healeth Thee." It helped me. The way she would personalize the words felt as though it was making it specifically for me. Jack watched and even learned the new way to sing the song, so that throughout our marriage, he could sing to me also. My mother talked me into going to the hospital, and Jack took me in. I can't recall if it was this time or later in our marriage that this happened again, but my colon had actually doubled in size due to block-age. It was serious pain, and many CF patients go through this.

A few years went by, and I found a good CF clinic. This one was good for a while, but eventually they started getting pushy with the same medications and being very harsh with me in a sudden manner that confused me. They knew I was only doing my basic treatments, and they were even encouraging me to keep it up since it was working. Then during one appointment, my doctor had me in the exam room alone and he said, "Vanessa, you are very sick. I hope you never plan on having children because your body just can't. You will die soon if you do not take this medication." I reminded him my name was Bethany and asked him what my PFT results were because I didn't feel like I was on death's door like he was suggesting. He held the paper to his face and said, "These numbers are very bad, Vanessa." I asked to see them, and he changed the subject and ended my appointment with, "Maybe you should go somewhere else." (Fun Fact: Even though I kept reminding the doctor of my name, he kept referring to me as Vanessa. I thought this was very strange, but later I looked up the meaning of the name Vanessa, and it means Butterfly. So naturally, me being me, I looked at this and said, "Okay, time to fly away." Maybe extreme, but I felt it was a sign.) It was the weirdest thing because this was my third or fourth visit with him, and the other times he had been so different. He would actually listen to me tell him about my body, what works and what I would prefer to do. My preferred choice was to not take these mega-harsh drugs that could be damaging my organs only for the temporary help they brought. Of course, for anyone with CF, you will most likely die young before the effects of all those drugs would even matter. But for me, someone with unshaken hope that I was going to live to be an old lady, side effects of medications really mattered to me. What used to be more of a choice because I just didn't want the burden or inconvenience of doing treatments became a more mature decision to try to preserve my organs as best I could. My mother was always huge on researching any drugs they would prescribe, and she would try to see if there was a natural supple-ment to help replenish the good things that often get affected in the body with heavy medications. But I was now calling all the shots, and if I didn't want to take them, I didn't have to. Big-girl-on-campus style. Obviously, no matter how mature and even rational my reasoning (I thought anyway), this would be so unfamiliar to my clinic, and eventually it would usher in a transition. This was both a relief but also discouraging because I just wanted them to listen to me about what I was feeling and why. This was the second clinic that didn't work out.

I left the clinic confused and hurt because I felt like in past visits, he had listened to me, and I liked him a lot. But here I was again, on my own, and back to my normal, simple treatments. If a sickness came and I felt I needed a boost besides the over-the-counter immune boosters, I would go to my primary and get an oral antibiotic. I did pretty well and even fought off pneumonia on my own without knowing it. I went to the doctor after a week of being very tired, and they did an X-ray and saw a small bit of pneumonia and said, "Well, that's all that's left. Looks like you fought it off. I'm going to give you some antibiotics to finish it." (Fun Fact: I noticed a dark spot in my intestines, so I asked him what it was. He said, "Oh, that's a fart." It was a great moment.)

If a CF doctor would have seen a spot of pneumonia, I would have been hospitalized for two weeks. For a young, married girl in her twenties, I was all about not being stuck in a hospital room, regardless of what would actually be best for me. This new life was great! But things wouldn't stay this smooth, because no matter how hard I tried to make CF just a background character, it seemed to keep trying to steal the spotlight.

I won't ever forget a night in November of 2014. We were in line to see a movie when all of a sudden, I couldn't breathe. Just Jack and Tearsa were with me, and thankfully both are used to plans getting unexpectedly messed up. Jack drove me to the hospital, and I held his hand and Tearsa's because I didn't know what was happening, and I was very scared. We went into the ER and all my vitals were pretty normal, but they brought me back, hooked me to fluids, and ran a few tests. Nothing! They diagnosed me with a severe panic attack. When my sputum culture came back, it did show some bacterial growth that I was familiar with, but it was never a huge deal when I "grew it" because CF doctors told me it really never goes away once it comes. However, when you are at a hospital with zero CF doctors, they tend to freak out over such a serious bacterial infection. They actually *asked* me if I needed to get a PICC line. I, of course, said, "Um, no." So they started meds through a regular IV, and I basically had to walk them through everything. They were shocked at my heart rate being so up and down after my albuterol treatments, which was normal for me. The doctor told me they were considering a pacemaker. "Yeah, no . . . we are not going to do that," I said. I left with some oral antibiotics to help my "panic attacks." It was nerve-racking to be under the care of doctors who were so unaware of CF procedures, but this is why there are clinics that can provide the proper care. However, I wasn't ready to give up the freedom I felt I had by not going to one. It was also nice to feel more in control because they didn't know how the cycle went, so I felt like I was calling the shots. No PICC? You'd better believe it. Another one down. Always hoping it was the last.

I was hospitalized a little after that due to being severely dehydrated. It was so bad I couldn't walk, and I was as white as a sheet. I looked so terrible that when I walked into the ER, they took me straight back. As the young man was trying to draw blood, I kept telling him I needed to get fluids first, but he was doing his job, even though my veins were not cooperating. I was getting dizzier, my hearing went out completely, I heard a loud ringing, and my head started nodding. He quickly picked me up, placed me in a wheelchair, and ran with me to the trauma unit while holding me in the chair with one hand and pushing my chair with the other. I continued to black out over and over. It was very scary, but I honestly remember feeling numb more than feeling fear. They finally got me fluids, and I went home that same day. Drink water folks. These quick hospital stays were more convenient for me and my busy life. But I was coming up on the hardest year of my life, and my little hospital pit stops were not going to cut it.

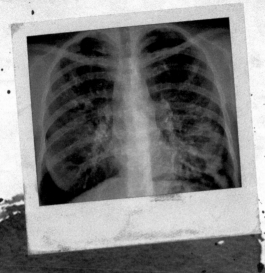

Midnight Miracle

The year began with the most incredible touch from God I have ever received. Jack and I throw a New Year's Eve party every year. We have no drinks stronger than coffee, and we even pray in the New Year. It's the highlight of our year because we get to see all our friends and eat Jack's life-changing smoked ribs! I had been feeling weak since that hospital stay in November. (Keep in mind, there was bacteria in my lungs not being treated at all during that time.) As I was enjoying the night, 11:45 p.m. came along, and I was catching up with my friend in the living room. "Bethany, are you feeling okay? You look a little pale." I assured him I was fine, but actually, I was struggling to remain attached to the conversation due to dizziness. "Your nose is bleeding!" he said.

I felt shocked at the news because that didn't happen often. I excused myself to my bedroom. I didn't want to bother Jack so he could continue to entertain the guests, so I just stood over my bathroom sink and tried to calm down and stop the bleeding. Well, it started bleeding harder. Still trying to keep it together for the house *full* of people trying to enjoy their night, I stuffed some toilet paper in my nose and turned on some worship music. I walked carefully to my bed and laid down on my right side with my phone beside me playing the music. I began to pray, asking God for peace in this moment as fear was really strong. I became weaker, and I couldn't even tell you if my nose had stopped bleeding because I began to feel something in the room change. It became a little cooler, and my eyes closed from exhaustion. "Peace. Jesus . . . give me peace." This was all I would say.

Now, people will say God does not speak to us. Maybe God does not speak to some, but I have felt His words become engraved into my very being, and they never leave me. "I will heal you, or I will take you. If those are the only options, what do you have to be afraid of?" He said this to me in my spirit. It wasn't like when He spoke confirming Jack to me when I turned around looking for who spoke in my ear. However, it was just as clear. Wow, I had never looked at it that way. All these years, fear had been holding onto my back, just like in my dream, and now, God brought such a deep revelation through such simplicity. It was like He pulled back the curtain to reveal the wizard—a serious face-palm moment.

There is no fear when you are in God's perfect will. Either way this could turn out, I win. He is ultimately my author and finisher. My beginning and my end. All I am required to do is obey His commands and live my life as close to His direction as possible. (Author's Addition: I have learned that as I draw closer to God and learn who He is as Father, Son, and Holy Spirit, I learn who I am, and I desire to serve Him because it's literally the least I can do after all He has done and continues to do for me! Obedience is not a bondage for me; it's a privilege! Surrender is not a burden to me; it's freedom!)

Within a second, my heart began to soak in His words. I started to feel my heart slowing down, then it stopped. But there was no fear. My lungs slowly quit breathing, and I just laid there, in the shell of a body that had stopped working. It was like time was no more. But nothing was happening, just peace. Suddenly, I felt as if my body was being pressed into the bed just for a moment, then I felt as if I was lifted off the bed completely. I was unable to open my eyes during this whole experience. After I was laid back down, it was as if a switch had been flipped on. Like when you trip a breaker and you have to go flip it back on, and just like that, my heart and lungs were working. But these were not the same lungs.

Normally breathing takes effort for me. If I am busy doing something, it won't be long until my lungs remind me that they need my attention, and I have to stop what I'm doing to help them breathe deeply. I can feel when there is a heavy amount of mucus the same way you can tell there is pulp in your straw when you drink. It gets harder to inhale, and that's when I pat my congested side and try to unclog the airway. Sometimes it works, sometimes it doesn't, and I continue to try to inhale, but I can't get air in. My fingernails turn a little blue, and I get lightheaded and need to sit down. I might even need to get someone to help me pat the backside of my lung to get it out. The students at my job, and even the older children who came to the day-care, have seen me do this many times, and so many of them ask me if they can "help me live" by patting me. They really are doing exactly that. My lungs also give a little jerk at the end of my breath at times, and if you stand close to me, you will hear the crackle sound coming from my throat. These are the lungs battling Cystic Fibrosis, but now—these were different lungs.

I didn't have to make these breathe; it was as if they were working for me, not me working for them. No crackle sounds coming from my throat. I was completely frozen in awe, just lying in my bed on my right side, soaking this all in. My lungs were breathing! THEY WERE REALLY BREATHING! At some point during this, some of my core support that was at our party began to fill up the room. Jack came beside me; my sister, Tearsa, at my feet; my sister-in-law holding my hand and her fiancé at the time (husband now) holding her. My dear friend, Jeweli, and her fiancé at the time (husband now), Nic, were sitting on the side of my bed, and my friend, Jonathan, on my other side. I had all of them worried at first, and I'm sure me crying and saying, "No way!" over and over had them confused. They had no idea what they had just walked in on. I was feeling healed lungs. I told them I could really breathe, and, of course, everyone cried, and we all laughed at me yelling "No WAY!" over and over. I was in such amazement! I so wish you could feel what I felt because it was beyond reality; it was indeed supernatural.

It was about to turn midnight, and I called my parents, Jack's parents, Pastor Chris, and many others who had walked this journey with me and told them I had been healed! We all celebrated in my bedroom with tears and amazement. They all went out to light the fireworks, but I wanted to stay in the room because God was still there, and I wasn't about to leave that Presence I felt. A few more friends of mine visited my room, and I just kept breathing and praising God. He also placed another milestone word in my spirit. He said, "Doctors can't fix you. Medicine can't fix you. Only I can fix you." I will never forget that feeling or those words which made my break-through possible. I needed those words He spoke to fight off that demon-ic-like fear that had bound me. I put that entire experience and the feelings I felt on "repeat" in my mind and heart, and I held tight to them because I was stepping into a season of unbelievable pain, loss, and humbling.

The next Sunday, my pastor asked me to come up on stage and give my testimony. I felt the power of God all over me as I spoke. I remember I began almost preaching about the crippling stronghold of fear, and the church erupted with "Amens." I guess I had doubts in my heart because I said, "I'm being healed." I don't know why I would say that unless there was a question in me about the completion of my miracle. At that point, I was still breathing very clear. That evening, I went to Orlando with my parents and sister; Jack was on the worship team. Through the night, I began to struggle to breathe. You can imagine how many thoughts and questions flooded my mind.

The next day at work, I found myself in the bathroom having a coughing fit and leaning over the trash can, watching the mucus hit the can along with many, many tears. I thought to myself, "Why? Why are these bad lungs back? What did I do to lose my healing? What will everyone think of me?" I have always promised God I would never get angry with Him since that time on my parent's couch. I may get confused, but I will not get angry. Eventually, I felt not only sick, but worse than I did before my miracle. So, I went back on my treatments of albuterol and saline. I tried to not cough at church or show how sick I was in fear of them thinking I was the biggest liar ever. Who would believe the other option, that God took back my healing? I couldn't even believe that myself. I was very confused, but also tried to talk myself into thinking, "Well . . . maybe this was a taste of what I can look forward to!" This mindset helped me get through the temporary disappointment, because now it was like, "Okay, God, I know what I am missing out on now. I WANT THOSE LUNGS BACK!"

Now we were back to where we were, just the bare minimum medications and no clinic to run to if things got bad. Another hospital pit stop came and went. They loaded me up on some IV antibiotics to get through a tough moment. It was like trying to throw a blanket over flames. Eventually I would need more help to keep this fire from consuming everything. To make things worse, I was basically forced into no medication because my dog hit my nebulizer off the couch and those things are not cheap when you have no insurance. I took that as a sign from God and just went without anything. I made it through another year. Here comes 2016.

The Hardest Year Yet

n May, my sweet friend, Jeweli, was getting married, and I was asked to be a bridesmaid. You can only hide how you feel so long until eventually it shows despite what you want. Jeweli was in the room with me on New Year's Eve; she was an eyewitness. I felt like I had to stay positive for her on her special day and hide my confusion and pain. She looked up to me as an example of faith. She cheered for me when I was healed; I couldn't let her in on the disappointment I felt. It was an outdoor wedding, and it took absolutely everything in me to walk down that aisle because I was so weak. Standing up there, I prayed under my breath that I would remain standing and breathing instead of blacking out, falling over, and ruining her day. Thankfully, God gave me the strength to not only stand there for her but to even dance a little at the reception. (I have the best moves by the way. Check my social media if you don't believe me.)

A day or so later, I went to the ER and was admitted into the hospital. Again, it was not a Cystic Fibrosis-friendly hospital, and in my defense, I didn't know where any were because I was not going to clinic like I was supposed to. My cultures and X-rays showed double pneumonia in both lungs and three different types of bacterial infection as well. Basically, a party was going on and everyone got an invite. They ran strong IV antibiotics for nine days. On the day they were going to release me, a pulmonary specialist decided to show up. She told me that the *Pseudomonas* (the bacterial infections they were seeing) needed to be treated further before I left, meaning she wanted me to stay another week. I left without being properly discharged, which meant I walked out without the medication they had been treating me with. Not smart at all, but I was young and able to make these choices on my own, and Jack didn't know any better to stop me. I was glad to be out of there feeling a tad bit better.

After a while, I was back to having horrible pain and as weak as could be. There were several times when I felt like giving up, but my family would beg me not to stop fighting, and I remembered God's words. It wasn't about me. I had a moment where I laid in my husband's arms and told him I felt so sick and I wasn't sure I would wake up if I fell asleep. I remember the fear and faith both in his eyes, feeling totally helpless as he was doing as I asked him to by just being beside me and holding me. I said, "God, if you are not going to heal me . . . then take me." Jack and I cried, and we eventually fell asleep holding each other. Then I woke up, and I was excited I was still with Jack but also sad to still feel such pain. It's a complicated emotion to explain.

In the middle of this emotional and physical battle, it was time for National Arts Festival, which was a highlight of my year. I had been coaching my teams through all this, as I had since 2012. This time, it was Tearsa's last year as a competitor, so it was important to me to push through the pain and be there for her. Nationals were held in Kentucky, so even though I felt weak and horrible, I packed my bags and went alongside Jack and my family. This is another pivotal moment in my life that I will never forget.

We were driving through the night as a whole church, and Jack, Tearsa, and I were on one of the smaller church vans because they are not as loud.

There were several others on the van with us. It must have been really late because everyone in the van was asleep. We had just hit some elevation in Tennessee, and I had my back to Jack as I was trying to get comfortable enough to sleep a little. I coughed a somewhat small cough, and it was productive, so I reached for my napkin and spit it out, noticing the consistency was very different. The van was pitch black other than the occasional streetlights flying by. I looked down and realized it appeared dark. I turned my phone flashlight on and looked at the napkin; it was blood. No mucus, just dark, red blood.

What I felt in that moment can only be described as slow-motion panic. I tried my hardest to stay fairly quiet for those sleeping on the bus while turning to Jack and waking him up in an absolute panic. He looked at it and instantly held me and began to pray in the Holy Spirit. Sorry if you don't believe in that, but in moments like this, you have no words and need the deepest form of intercession. Jack and I believe that's praying in the Spirit. Suddenly, my entire chest began to gurgle, and I felt as if I was drowning. I coughed again and another handful of blood came up. I just laid there with my face in my praying husband's neck thinking, "Please God. Don't have me die like this." There was nothing we could do but pray. My sister could hear Jack praying, and she began to quietly lift me up. My mother, who was following us in her car, texted me saying, "I don't know what's happening right now, but I'm praying." How wild is that? She knew by the Spirit. A momma just knows. That mother's intuition? It's called the Holy Spirit in my professional, unprofessional opinion. As I laid there, gurgling in my chest because of what I can only imagine was blood, I was drowning, and in the middle of what should have been such a fear-filled moment . . . a wave of peace came over me. There was absolutely no fear. I was gurgling loud enough for Jack to hear it. I remember thinking how much I just didn't want to die like that.

In minutes, the gurgling stopped, and I coughed up just mucus. Not even a hint of blood. I put my head on Jack's shoulder and thanked him for praying and took a sigh of relief that we "made it through another time." No one on the van knew about it except us and my sister. When we arrived at nationals, I was supposed to be a room leader like I always had been, but I was so sick I wanted to be with someone who could take care of me if I needed them to. My parents were going to have to stay at a different hotel because my pastor was told there were no more rooms available (plus they were very expensive). My mother asked my father to contact one of my aunts who always said to contact her if we needed anything. So, he did, and God moved! We got a handicap suite in the same hotel as the church, which was huge, with a little living room and all. On top of that, she also told me to order room service as many times as I wanted. I cried and cried at how great God was. I was able to spend so much time with my precious mother who I always want beside me when I'm sick.

The church had a gathering to eat and do a small service, and Pastor Chris asked me to come, and they all lifted me up in prayer. It was a big moment for me because I was always trying to hide the sickness now for the second time in my life because I was so worried of what they would think since I spoke of my miracle happening. But there I was so weak I couldn't stand in front of everyone. My endless humble pie consumption wasn't over because it was time to show up at Arts Festival like this. The event that made me "somebody": the place where people asked to take pictures with me because they had watched me on my YouTube channel or in person at previous festivals. Here I was at Arts Festival in a wheelchair being pushed around by my family because I couldn't even walk. People came up and talked to me, asking what happened or if I could take a picture with them. It was so hard to smile, and just talking would make me lightheaded. I had so many ask to pray for me. Of course, I said yes.

As we were leaving one of my sister's performances, which Jack and I coached, a man chased my mother (who was pushing me), my sister, and I out of the room. He said, "God kept pressing me to come give you a word. I was going to wait till the next performance was over, but He wouldn't let me. The word is *reverse*. He's going to reverse it." My mother began to cry and said God also told her years ago that He was going to reverse the diagnosis. This man happened to be the head of our PEN FL district, and it was super neat to meet him and get a picture. (Fun Fact: The piece that year, which we coached my sister in, was called *Paralyzed*. It was ironic that I was in a wheelchair during the festival and her performance.) I spent a lot of time in the hotel room with my mother as she rubbed essential oils all over my feet and made me drink plenty of water, and of course, walked around the room praying and worshiping Jesus for her daughter's healing. She felt God say He was doing "a new thing," and she would begin singing a rather annoying little ditty that went, "God is doin' a new thing. You know He's doin' it." We would all laugh and beg her to stop. But I wanted to believe her and the word I received.

On August 8 we arrived home, and I got much worse. I was doubled over in pain, and my father got me an SpO finger monitor. I put it on and it read 82%. (Normal is 100%.) My mom cried and begged me to go to the hospital. I told her they didn't know how to treat Cystic Fibrosis at the local hospitals. My father researched CF specialists and a place came up. It was a bit of a drive, but it would be worth it to finally be in the right hands. We called Jack, who was on the worship team that morning, and told him to meet us at the hospital. When we arrived, they had to wheel me in and take my vitals. My SpO was 80%, and when I would say anything, it would drop into the 70s. Immediately, they rushed me to the trauma unit, and the damage control began. Instantly, I had an IV in each arm, blood being drawn, stickers being stuck, blood pressure cuff going on, oxygen going in. The foot traffic was unreal. Then they began to check my organs to ensure they were still all working; I had never even thought about that. The room was packed, and I knew my mother was worried but was in deep prayer for her "Bunny," so I just kept my eyes on her and made sure she could see my smile through the flood of doctors and nurses. My smile communicated to her that I was going to be okay. I had peace. One of the doctors told me, "You are one very sick girl."

He explained to me that they had a fantastic team of Cystic Fibrosis doctors who would meet me in the morning. I let out a sigh of relief, because for the first time in so long, I was going to be taken care of by the right physicians.

I met the CF team, and they assured me they were going to help get me back on track, but that would mean me taking my health seriously, and I agreed. The time of pretending was over. I had got down to the sickest I had ever been, and I never wanted to get to that place again. Thankfully, they didn't push for me to get a PICC line because I really hate those. However, I did have to have three antibiotics through my IV. I also had to have breathing treatments twice a day along with airway clearance. That could mean being patted by hand or someone using an instrument called a procussor (something like a massager that vibrates very intensely, and the respiratory therapist moves it all around my lung area while I do my nebulized treatments). They also have a machine that is a nebulizer, and as your medication goes in, it expands your lungs by shooting it in super-fast. That one hurts me a little, and I do not like it. There is also the vest that you put on and it vibrates like crazy. This one works the best I would say, but it always gave me a huge headache. I did it all, and it amazes me how many forms of airway clearance there are. When I was a teen, I only remember patting with hands by a respiratory therapist. Medical advancements are incredible. Thank you, Jesus, for these ingenious inventions.

My hospital stay was, you guessed it, two weeks long, which was enough time to get the same nurse a few times and meet just about everyone on the floor. I had some of the greatest nurses. One would come in and sing the worship songs with me that I had on repeat. One day, I got a really severe nose bleed out of nowhere and was freaking out, and this nurse came rushing into my room, got on my bed, and held a tissue on my nose, pinching it closed, and began speaking scriptures and praying to God for me. She told me, "Have faith and just believe." I was in such shock. I had never experienced something even close to this, but I loved it. I remember closing my eyes and letting her lift me up as I rested in the peace that flooded my room.

Many more amazing things happened. One nurse was named Emmanuel and I would say, "God is with me!" when he would come in. He saw me drinking a Boba tea one day and asked me all about my favorite flavor, and on his day off, he went and bought me and Jack a Boba tea and brought it to us. I was actually enjoying my hospital stay because I was surrounded by the best people. They had several therapy services that they offered those who were staying in the hospital for a long time, and one of those was massage therapy. Andrew, my massage therapist, was so great! We told him all about human videos and showed him some of our videos (*Paralyzed* Small Human Video; go watch it if you haven't already), and he was amazed and said he understood the story. We got to share about God and our faith walk and had some great conversations with him. They also sent me music therapy, which was usually a guy with an acoustic guitar who would come in and ask if I had any requests. I always would ask him to play some hymns, and the presence of God would come right in as we worshiped.

Two weeks went by so quickly, and my doctors were surprised daily with my quick recovery. I gained five pounds in one day. From the moment I was admitted, the doctors were always surprised at how clear my lungs sounded when they listened with the stethoscope. Also, my IV remarkably lasted the longest they could let it, which I believe was six days according to their rules, then they had to give me a new one which lasted the rest of my visit. Overall, it was so great to be taken care of and get my health back on track. In fact, my doctor said, "We need to get the train back on track so we can start pushing it forward till it can run on its own." That was the plan. I was released back into the wild and went back home with a passion for doing all I could to prove to my new CF team that I wanted to get better and with a husband who literally soaked up all he could about CF and the medications the two weeks we both were there. That's right, Jack stayed with me day and night the whole time.

When I went back for my follow-up appointment, they talked me into starting a nebulized CF medication. As you remember, this had always been a sore subject with me. This medication's job is to break down extracellular DNA by acting like an enzyme naturally found in the lungs. By doing this, it helps the normally thick mucus my lungs produce become thinner and looser. Almost every CF patient gets on this medication. It can lead to a few side effects such as a change in voice, which a bunch of my CF friends have experienced. They had to tell me that a side effect of this drug is potential lung bleeds. I wasn't too thrilled about taking this drug, but I was willing to try it.

In October, I was on the new medication and weighing about 110 lb. I did very well, and my lung function began to climb. It seemed like things were on the up! Then the end of November came along. I started coughing up a bunch of thick, green mucus and had a fever of 100° for several days. I tried all the natural remedies I knew of: essential oils and a honey, flour, and coconut oil paste rubbed on the chest to help congestion. Maybe it worked, but not enough. Back to the hospital I went.

It was December 7, and I was not emotionally or mentally prepared for what was about to happen. This doctor was different than the one who saw me in the hospital. My lung function was exactly one number less than it was in the hospital, and I had lost five pounds. My SpO was registering at 86, so they placed me on oxygen until the end of my appointment. Then my doctor hooked me to a monitor and made me speed walk through the halls for about six minutes. He grew more concerned when my heart rate went up to 130 BPM. He said many patients whose oxygen was that low have their hearts working double-time. He also said that many people in my condition don't make it to the hospital before going into heart failure. Then he proceeded to tell me that I would need to be on an oxygen tank for the rest of my life, and I would eventually have adult CF-related diabetes. From what I understand, this is when the mucus causes scarring of the pancreas, but the pancreas still makes insulin—just not enough. Monitoring and insulin shots are required. Literally just another layer of junk to add to the glorious poo cake of CF. He also said I had the lungs and heart of an elderly person, which was kind of rude of him, but I'm over it now. As long as when I'm old, I have the heart and lungs of a young person!

As he was saying all of this, I was just looking at him, trying to hold back all my feelings, but I couldn't help but break down and cry. I shared with him how much hearing all that hurts me when I'm trying to do my very best to take everything I need to, but it's like fighting a losing battle. As I shared my heart with him in an emotional and raw way, I noticed his eyes started filling with tears, and he said, "I'm so sorry I can't just fix you." Instantly, I remembered the word God gave me in 2015: "Doctors can't fix you. Medicine can't fix you. Only I can fix you." I took a deep breath and was able to convince my doctor to let me stay out of the hospital for Thanksgiving, but I had to agree to do my nebulized treatments including my normal albuterol and saline three times a day, take my CF nebulized medication twice a day, take two oral antibiotics, *and* work with my insurance to try to get an oxygen tank. I was trying to prove to my new team that I was dedicated to their plans to help me get better! I absolutely was so appreciative of them and their efforts. Even if the news was overwhelming and the delivery a little harsh, I knew it was only to help me!

So much was on my mind during the forty-five-minute ride home. I called my Uncle Scott, who throughout my life has been an extended voice of God for me. I told him about all that was said, and he said the doctors are like actors in a play reciting their script, treating me as they have been taught. There is a system basically. A strategic battle plan drawn up to fight the many battles CF brings. Yes, it's hard to hear so much negativity when all my life I have spoken health and healing over myself, but this is the reality of CF. Without my faith in healing, I promise you, I would have given up. Many who battle CF also struggle with depression, and I totally know why! Having to be told constantly all the ways your body is broken. Not just one thing, many things. My heart goes out to the entire CF community that has been doing this without God. It's hard enough with faith. But I knew God was in this, like He always has been.

I later received a call saying my CAT scan results from my appointment showed mucus plugging—the first time it could be seen—and pneumonia . . . again. They agreed to let me stay out for Christmas as long as I didn't feel any worse and my fever didn't climb. The day after I got the news, I had a dream. In the dream, I signed up for a race. It was an enormous obstacle course in a nature setting, much like that movie with all the boys and one girl who run through the maze. (See how I did that. Hashtag avoiding name dropping so I can't get like sued or something.) I was getting ready to start when I noticed my mother-in-law cheering me on. I took off running, and I could feel my lungs breathing so effortlessly. Eventually, I noticed there was more to this race. There was an enemy whose goal was to tag me before I tagged them. As long as I touched them first, they would disappear. I noticed they were dressed like a certain nationality, which was strange, but I was dodging them left and right.

Eventually, I ran right into an open battlefield, and in the distance, I saw hundreds of them coming after me. Without an ounce of fear in me, I let out a battle cry and took off full speed toward the enemy, who were coming after me with all their might. When we met, it was like a scene from a superhero movie! I was ducking, dodging, and tagging so quickly that they couldn't get me first. As I approached the end of the race, I noticed my mother-in-law, cheering again. I then got my score because it was a race, and my dream was over. I woke up encouraged by the effortless feeling of running. I later received some clarity from God through Uncle Scott: the reason I saw that particular nationality was because in that nation, when anyone refuses the treatments the doctors give them, they are labeled basically dead to them and they can no longer get medical help. This would make total sense to me in a few years. (Author's Addition: When you receive what you believe is a prophetic dream, be sure you write it down. For me, when my dream has been prophetic, it feels different from a normal, dumb dream. First of all, it isn't at all dumb. Now, there is sometimes a little humor mixed in, but a prophetic dream feels like I'm living it. It's real to me. I remember details and all my senses are used normally. So, it's truly like being there. *Write down your dreams!* Pray to God to bring you clarity, and I suggest seeking wise, godly counsel on an interpretation if it is not revealed to you fully, and even if it is, double confirmation and a different perspective is always good! Be careful who you share your dreams with.)

CRUTCHES

n December 2016, we had my immediate family over. My sister and I cooked as my father and Jack watched football. Our mother hung around the kitchen, telling us what to do here and there, but she never was much for cooking, which worked out perfectly because Tearsa would and still does kick us out of the kitchen anyway! While we were opening presents, I went to my bedroom to grab something. While there, I had an incredible idea. When I was a child during the Christmas season, the ballet company I was with would always go to nursing homes and churches and dance. My cousin would do a dance to the song "Breath of Heaven," and I loved this song so much that I would often put on my own performance for my parents in the living room. The moment I had this idea, I wanted to do it for them, but next year so that Tearsa could sing it, and I could buy a costume and make it real nice. As I was thinking about this, God told me, "Do it now. Next year things will be different." I didn't question it. I came out into the living room and asked them to sit on the couch, and I started the music. It was as if a heavy spirit was lifted in me and in the room as we all cried. I remembered almost every movement with God's words heavy on my mind. I knew I needed to take in this moment.

January came, and I had a visit to my primary care doctor, hoping for just an oral antibiotic to get me feeling better again. However, as soon as they listened to my lungs, she said she heard no airflow in my left lung and strongly advised me to be admitted. We went to the ER where I could be seen by my CF team. In the ER, my vitals showed no real sign for alarm. My SpO was 95%, and my heart rate was in the low 100s. They did hear movement in my left lower lung, but very little. They put me in for a two-week stay and started an IV antibiotic to help control the bacterial growth. They also decided to start me on another nebulized medication. This medication is used to help stop the growth of the ever-annoying *Pseudomonas aeruginosa* and is a staple drug in the CF community.

The first few days got me feeling down. It felt like we just went through this, and here I was again. I opted out of the PICC again, so I was praying my IV would stick it out like last time! I had mountain-top moments and valley moments while I was in there. The new medication seemed to make me breathe deeper, and I began to cough up brown mucus, which they told me was older stuff, so that was a good sign. It meant it was getting all the way down into the deeper lobes of my lungs. They had taken a sputum culture the day I arrived, and a few days later, the results came in. It showed that where there used to be three forms of *Pseudomonas*, there was now just one. I was so excited that I, of course, posted the news on Facebook, praising God first then my own dedication to taking care of myself by doing my treatments and even taking some natural things to help. Such a great, mountain-top, strong faith moment, right?

Well, my doctors came in and informed me that even though the cultures don't grow it, it doesn't mean it isn't there. I fought to remain hopeful in the thought that it really was gone. Then the next report came in and showed another growth. I told myself, "But that's just two, keep your head up, Bethany." I was trying so hard to not be swallowed by defeat. One doctor said my left lung sounded better; one heard no difference. They agreed to place me on a 24-hour antibiotic drip for the remainder of my stay, which at this point was a little over a week and a half to go. That's a ton of medication for me. My family came to visit me many times, and my sister made up this character called "The Intern." The character description was that she was interning at my hospital but knew nothing on how to work anything. She brought me so much laughter and joy; I really needed that. (Side Note: You can see these videos on my YouTube channel and laugh too; she is amazing.) The young ladies at my church made me a big strawberry shortcake, and Jack, of course, stayed with me the whole time, only leaving to grab us food.

However, one day, he was really having a hard time being stuck in that one room. He went home to wash our clothes, and I told him just to sleep there for the night. After he kissed me goodbye and slowly left my room with the door closing behind him, I instantly felt such fear and sadness flood me. *I'm alone in this right now. What if something happens to me and Jack can't get here in time? Who can hold me and pray?* I had so many reasons to feel afraid. Thankfully, God sent me a respiratory therapist for my nighttime treatments, and he was a hardcore Christian. He asked if he could pray for me, and, of course, I said "Yes." His prayer was all about peace. When he left, I felt so much better. I just played my worship music and prayed until I fell asleep from exhaustion. My IV lasted the full fourteen days! They kept it extra-clean and let me keep it the whole time, and I was so glad.

On the day they sent me home, my PFT was the highest it had been in a long time and I was 100 lb. After my release, I started jogging a little and felt like it was really helping. I remember going to an outdoor track to run with Jack, and I would walk the curves and run the rest. I would look up into the sunset sky, and I said with tears in my eyes from the strain, "Jesus, help me do this," as I pushed myself to run to the next curve. There is something special that happens when you truly act on Philippians 4:13. I was taking my nebulized medications, and I was drinking chocolate extra-calorie drinks to bump up my weight. February 8 came, and it was time for my follow-up appointment. Lung function was up and so was weight gain; things looked good! These appointments were rare, so we celebrate them.

In March, Jack and I both fought what felt like the flu, so I called my doctors and told them my symptoms. They prescribed me a beast of an antibiotic that was 750mg. The moment I took it, I felt terrible, but I tried to keep with it for at least a few days. I just couldn't, so I tried to use some raw garlic, which I had heard was a natural antibiotic. I almost instantly felt better. I went on April 19 for a routine visit and my lung function had dropped a bit, so they prescribed me an oral antibiotic that I had taken in the past. They also got me back on a nebulized medication and told me to take up to five chocolate calorie drinks a day.

I was finally living life as a normal Cystic Fibrosis patient, which included several hours of breathing treatments a day, going to routine appointments, and being hospitalized for lung infections the same time in the year like clockwork. This became my life, but I wasn't about to stop hoping and praying for my healing. I was at the altar at my church one night, and a woman I had never seen before came over to me and said into my ear, "God loves it when you dance daughter. Don't stop dancing." I knew this was from God, because no one knew that dance is my intimate form of worship to Jesus. I always dance in my living room with the worship music on full blast when I'm home alone. I would often push past what my body could handle to praise Him, then I'd collapse on the couch for a few minutes to have a coughing session. There is a special anointing that comes over me when I dance for Him. This anointing goes all the way back to my childhood. I am so thankful my parents didn't keep me from doing things like dance lessons because I was "frail" or because of the germs. I used to dance to so many worship songs. I remember one where we stretched our arms out and acted like we were soaring with wings like eagles! There was also one where we took steps forward and stood up tall as the song sang, "I stand, I stand in awe of You." Then, we would bow to Jesus. I loved dance. I dance through the storm.

During this time, I walked through a different type of storm. My mother started acting different. My parents have walked through many trials, and some of those have brought distrust between them. I remember sitting on the couch with my mother as she voiced her heart to me. She started crying uncontrollably, and I had to hold her as she sobbed. Those of us in the room were taken back by this, and unfortunately, it was the first heartbreaking event with many more to follow.

As things progressed, we took her to the doctor, and they diagnosed her with perimenopause. Things eventually led to her not wanting to eat or take care of herself, which resulted in her losing weight very quickly. Sad discussions had to take place on what to do to help her. There was talk of mental health facilities, hospitalization with feeding tubes to get her nutrition, and even the possibility of Baker Acting. We didn't want to do any of these, but she needed to get better, and we just kept going back and forth on what to do.

We took her to the ER and told them of her drastic weight loss. They checked out the normal things, took her blood, and did an EKG. They said she was fine, and they couldn't help her. This tore us up as a family, because she was always the strong one. Eventually, she was skinnier than me and refusing to shower, so her skin was very dry. She was only eating one meal a day, a chicken sandwich with two large fries from the Lord's chicken place, yes, that one! This was a relief to us because she was eating nothing before. She wouldn't leave the house, not even on her birthday. She moved into her own room in the house and refused to let us in unless it was to take her bedding to wash it. She would lie to us about things like washing and eating. She would cry and beg me not to leave the house when I would come to visit, and it hurt me to the core. Emotional trauma for all of us. This was far from the woman who raised me. But one thing that didn't change was her love for Jesus.

One day, I was visiting, and I started singing a worship song. I looked behind me, and my little, weak-looking mother had her hands raised and tears pouring down her face in worship, spiritually strong! There she was, that's my mommy. I hated that this was happening to her, but I am so happy she is still with us.

My father, Jack, and I went to eat with Uncle Scott, and he gave me a word. He said, "The Lord says, I am removing all your crutches." He further explained that this meant that I would have only God to lean on. A crutch helps you keep the pressure off the injury so you can heal. Could my faith in my mother's faith be a crutch? Or could my mother in general be a crutch? There were times I would lean on her and her faith and let mine take a back seat, meaning I would rest while she prayed for me and fought for me. But there were also times I felt I placed her motherly concerns for me above my commands from God. I really wasn't sure what this word meant, but so many possibilities ran through my head. What I was supposed to do with this word was to take it to the Lord in prayer and ask Him what I needed to do! But instead of surrendering my crutches through prayer, I just kept figuring things out on my own. My mother is going through this, because she's a crutch of mine, and she had to be removed. The big problem with this is, the enemy can use this as ammo to bring guilt and condemnation toward myself, or I could blame my father's actions and that can bring bitterness, or I could get mad at God for allowing it to happen and turn away from Him! So many ways this could go!

Give these situations you can't begin to understand right to God, because only He knows the whole story. Because I did not know then what I know now, this word from God worried me instead of calling me to my knees. I began to try to diagnose my own crutches at times. Jack also received the same word that day at dinner. God was removing his crutches. I asked him what his were, and he told me he wasn't sure.

The CF Script

n the middle of 2017, another CF medication was added to my treatment list, which again was targeting the *Pseudomonas* bacteria. Thankfully, it came with its own machine and took only two minutes to do a treatment. I did well on this medication, so we added it to the list. I would alternate between the two which targeted that specific bacteria. Twenty-eight days on one, then twenty-eight days on the other, but never without either. I was still doing my bronchial dilator, saline, the medication which helped clean up the lungs, and my digestive enzymes and multivitamins. Working hard to get better.

At my clinic visit, we were told some pretty amazing news. There was a new medication which targeted the mutated gene itself. These types of medications have proven to be super beneficial and the closest thing yet to a cure. They told me that both of my gene mutations qualified for this miracle drug, which works to help the "gates" stay open longer, allowing more chloride ions to move in and out of the cells. This potentially helps the balance of salt and water in the lungs. My team was ecstatic that I qualified, and so was I! This could be a huge answer to our prayers. We told the team we wanted to move forward on this.

Only a couple days later, as I was staying home from work due to major back pain, my nurse called me as I was praying about this new breakthrough treatment. She said, "Bethany, I have some terrible news. They made changes to the qualifications and you no longer qualify." On top of that news, she told me my sputum cultures showed double growth of *Pseudomonas*—even with all these nebulized medications that are supposed to be targeting that bacteria. It seemed I just couldn't catch a break. It was a very disappointing phone call. I went to visit my mom, and I told her about the whole thing. She grabbed my hands as I was crying, and she said to me, "Everything is going to be okay." I completely believed her. She placed her hands on my back and began to pray over my lungs. I needed her so much. It was like having her back for a small moment. I felt peace. Jack and I prayed together, and it was as if God reminded me that medication would not get the glory. This was bigger than that. My disappointment faded quickly, and I continued praying for the real cure.

Right around this time, Jack and I were getting ready to be Mary and Joseph for our church's Christmas production for the eighth year in a row, but this time, I felt something powerful happening. I had a scene where I was holding baby Jesus, who was a real baby every year, and my lines hit me like a strong wave. It was like I was saying each word to the face of my Savior who would eventually die on the cross for me, and who would speak to me in such a way that would keep me fighting for my healing that He paid for. I could barely get the words out, and thankfully, almost my whole church knows my story and could cry along with me, so it wasn't like I messed up the production. That was a very emotional moment happening in a very humbling way—right there in front of everyone. I can't forget the feeling I had.

Ironically, the winter began to be the hardest season to stay out of the hospital for me. The pneumonia and flus that came through were becoming more and more difficult to dodge. Working with children always worried my doctors; I wouldn't dare tell them I let the children hug on me and even get in my face sometimes as they talk to me. Honestly, I rarely even thought about germs when they were with me. I was very happy when my father-in-law merged the daycare ministry with the private school. I was moved from diapers to kindergartners, which was not a huge improvement in the germ department, but it did sound better to my doctors. Unfortunately, being near children day after day constantly proved to be a bad idea, and soon I was moved to the front desk. This was perfect for me! I could still greet everyone as they came and answer calls all day long without as much risk.

Eventually, I created friendships with the parents of our students, and they still remain some of my biggest supporters. It was really a God-ordained position for me. School was always such a horrible reminder of how badly I struggled with learning, especially in math! Now I was encouraging each student to take their education seriously, patting them on the back daily, telling them they are smart and they *can do it*. Not only that, they have watched my good days and the days when it took everything in me just to stand up and hug them goodbye and tell them how much I loved them. They have learned much about Cystic Fibrosis, and you can often find one of them patting my back if they are near me during a coughing fit. They have prayed for me during our school chapel service. They prayed for new lungs for Mrs. Bethany. They have cried when I cried, laughed at my funny stories, and loved me with such a love that I never knew was possible. I care so deeply for my students, and many call me "Mom." I don't ever clock out from my "job." In fact, several of them message me through the weekends, and they know I am always here for them at any time. Our small private school is not just a school; it's primarily a ministry. I am so thankful to be able to freely talk about Jesus to them and show them His love daily!

People ask me if I have kids; I tell them I have about seventy-five. God has blessed me with the love of so many children of all ages, and because of their love, I have never felt a void in not having my own children yet. They are one of the main reasons I continue to fight this battle and not give up. I know they watch me and their hearts are invested in my story. I also know that when I smile through the pain, it gives them peace. They understand that I'm in Jesus' hands; He's taking care of me and I'm going to be okay. I don't let them see me get too low if I can help it, even on my worst days, because my attitude can change their attitude. As children, they are so moldable. Each day they may walk in with a new shape. It's my job to be part of the process of shaping them into godly men and women. They are all my babies. Even if they can see the weak body, they will never see the weak spirit.

I've often had my low moments, and then my unbelievable high moments. So many of these were in services at my church. I have gone through many phases through the years, like the season where, when special guest ministers would come, I would run to the altar to get prayed for. I'm not kidding you, almost 100% of the time, the minister would literally pray for everyone around me, and I would not be touched. I would get frustrated! I would think to myself, "Seriously, I bet I'm in way more of a desperate place in my life than all these people slain in the Spirit all around me." Not the right attitude to have I know, but I'm human! Then I was in a season where I thought to myself, "If I'm already healed by His stripes, I don't need to go up for healing."

Once, when I had this mindset, I was standing at the altar at a special service and the guest minister asked for those in need of healing to raise their hand. I had every intention *not* to, and yet my hand shot up as if someone had me by the wrist. My hand was completely limp, and I couldn't pull it down. I was pushed on stage by people around me and came face-to-face with this very intense-looking minister. I was very much against "falling out" unless it was a God thing. I hate being pushed or forced like some ministers have tried to do to me in the past. So, as he approached me, I took a stance to help me stay up and fight off the pushing I knew was coming. He noticed me bracing myself stubbornly, and he smiled at me and touched my head ever so gently. Right away, I started trembling, but not falling. He just stepped back and watched me with this grin on his face as if he knew my thoughts and wanted to watch that pride and stubbornness be exposed. Quickly I realized that falling would have been way less embarrassing. I looked just like those blow-up windsock things in front of car dealerships. I wished God would just let me face plant. After what felt like forever, I tried to walk myself off the stage, but the man of God came after me again, smiling. He touched my belly and so began round two. I learned my lesson that night—don't try to control how God touches you, and definitely don't fight it. Just let Him do it His way; who are you to think you have control over His move?

I would go through seasons where I was getting words and promises left and right through people, then times where I felt like I was totally abandoned by God and left in silence—in such pain and misery with no words or directions to follow. It was up and down. But remember, I made a promise to God that I would *never* be angry at Him. I kept that promise even through the hardest of times—like the dreadful hospital stay of 2018.

I had gone to my appointment on January 3 and they were very unhappy with my health. I was actually going in for my study drug appointment. (Side Note: Earlier in life and as a child, my parents never let me do studies because there were so many risks involved. I agreed to do this one because it was a drug I had been on before and they were combining it with another drug I was familiar with. I thought, "Why not?") When I went in, they were shocked at my weight loss, so they sent me over to the clinic. I was 89 lb. due to having no appetite for a month. The doctors urged me to be admitted into the hospital where the plan was to place a gastrostomy tube, which is placed directly into the abdomen and delivers nutrition directly into the stomach. This is actually very common for the CF community because of the crazy amount of calories we have to take in to maintain our weight. Almost 4,000 calories daily are needed to put on weight, which was almost impossible for me to do. As much as I didn't want to be skinny anymore, I really did not want to get a tube. I promised my doctors I would do everything I could to bring my weight up. I just needed them to give me one more chance. However, my fever stayed throughout the next night and day, and so Jack and I decided it was time to be hospitalized.

On January 4, as usual, it happened. Great start to the year. This would be *by far* the worst hospital stay yet. We kept this from my mother because of the condition she was in, but she eventually found out, of course. It started out with me going into the ER and being rushed into the trauma unit. They went to place the IV and blew my main big vein which was always "old faithful" and held the IVs the best. Now they had to fish for the little ones and ended up with one in my wrist, which was very painful. Test results came in during our thirty-six hour stay in that little trauma room. The report was far from good. In fact, it was the hardest report to hear. I had viral and bacterial pneumonia in my left lower lobe. I had a flu strand called RSV, a staph infection, mucus plugging so bad it was expanding my airways, and they told me my left lung was showing signs of deterioration and holes were developing. This news shook me, and I began to cry and felt so low in my spirit. But it didn't last long; I was soon back to my encouraging self—speaking scriptures and making Facebook updates as positive as I could.

They talked me into getting a PICC line because they had three antibiotics going at once and they couldn't all go through one IV. I would keep one in my IV and the other two going through my PICC. I agreed to the placement and went through the dreaded procedure. Eventually they got me into my own hospital room. The day after getting my PICC, I noticed my arm was twice its normal size. So, at 1 a.m., they took me to get a sonogram, which showed blood clotted around the tip of the PICC. Because of this, they decided to remove the PICC, but my nurse didn't know how, so she went and got a stat nurse who was about 100 years old and had no filter on his mouth. He got things started, but then decided to let this be a learning experience for my nurse. He let her pull it out as he told stories about his days in the service. The removal was good, but it came out totally clean—the blood clot was now floating in my veins. I was a touch freaked out by that, but they didn't seem to be. The stat nurse started another IV in my arm as he said, "Whoa, blood is squirting everywhere." I rolled my eyes and just prayed. They began to run a blood thinner through the IV, which was a first for me. As soon as she unclamped my IV, it began to go in, and my head felt super heavy, and my chest began heating up. I yelled for her to stop it, which she did. We waited a minute until I told her to try again. Still, I felt terrible. She said we would wait for the doctors to decide what to do.

A few hours later, my room was full of my CF team. Six doctors surrounded my bed, asking me how I was feeling. They then proceeded to drop a few more truth bombs on me. They were going to give me blood thinning shots and they had to go through all of the horrid possible reactions, like bleeding to death. No big deal, right? Any more news doc? Oh yeah, you also have adult CF-related diabetes; here is a booklet about how this will change your life, like finger pricks throughout the day and two shots in the belly morning and night. Also, you will need to watch your sugar; no more sweet tea is our suggestion! (Fun Fact: I am a sweet tea lover, and it is kind of close to an addiction.) But wait, that's not all! We also need you to consider writing your WILL and signing this paper saying that if you flat line, you want to be revived because there is a solid chance that the blood clot could hit your lungs and you will instantly stop breathing. My reaction: "Did you say no more sweet tea?" Just kidding; I actually just burst into tears. Jack sat in the little chair in the corner he had been sleeping in for days, and he was just as shocked and numb as I was.

The social worker who was part of my team knelt beside me and held my hand with tears in her eyes. She said, "It's too much, isn't it? I'm so sorry." The rest of the team left, knowing how much all that news hurt me, but unable to do anything to help make hearing it easier. I loved the team; they all cared so deeply. This disease is just so unforgiving. My social worker and Jack held me as I wept, trying to take in all this information about how broken my body was since the day I walked into the hospital on this particular trip. Holes in my lungs, clogged airways, viral and bacterial pneumonia, RSV flu, staph infection, feeding tube threats, PICC line failure, blood clots, diabetes, and death itself. That's just a lot. I'd like to think of myself as hard to knock down, but being punched in the face this many times had me weak in the knees. Was this it? Was I out for the count? I was fine for the next couple hours, and I was making a Facebook Live update with encouraging words for everyone. I'm sure my perseverance and fight are so frustrating to the devil. It even frustrates me sometimes! Even if I'm close to KO, I stand up, spit the blood out of my mouth, and keep swinging. Even when I think it's over, eventually a burst of energy and hope will arise. This is truly from God Himself.

When we left the hospital, I begged God to let this be the last time. I said to myself, "I never want to come back here." Then we hit up the Old Country Buffet on the way home, where I pigged out on some southern goodness and drank a bunch of SWEET TEA; it was glorious. I went home and tried to read the diabetes book, but honestly, I didn't care. I hated the idea of adding yet another thing to my regimen. I had my insulin pen that the hospital let me take home because I had zero insurance. It was just sitting on my dresser, and as I was thinking about this "new addition to my life," it just started leaking. Every bit of insulin ran out all over my dresser. Call me crazy, but I took that as a sign and never thought about diabetes changing my life in a long-term way again. At my next clinic visit, they sent in the diabetes doctor, and I politely told him I was not going to take the insulin and gave him my blood sugar meter with all my tests saved for two weeks without insulin. Since the numbers were not at a dangerous level, he respected my decision and left the room. The rest of the appointment went well. My weight was up enough to take the G-tube off the table. Things seemed to be okay, for now.

The harsh truth of Cystic Fibrosis is, you just never know how you're going to feel the next day. I was balancing life as an adult CF patient, full-time employee at my father-in-law's private school, part-time Arts Festival coach at my church, and also trying to find time to enjoy life with Jack. I stayed busy—just how I liked it, making each day count. But things were about to get on a whole new level.

A Crazy Step of Faith

My Story Continues...

n July 2018, Jack and I went with his family to Campmeeting in Cleveland, Tennessee again. I really look forward to these meetings because God always moves in my own life as well as Jack's. Our family has the privilege of doing the youth services that take place in the mornings, then we join the main sanctuary for the evening services. You talk about long—these services can go for hours, and they are every day, twice a day, for over a week. These services are saturated with the Holy Spirit, and the heritage of the anointing is so tangible. On Wednesday, July 4th, it was my father-in-law's morning to preach. We as a family sang a worship song. Yes, they have me sing with them, and I usually do a drama solo. It's a great time of ministry as a family.

One night, a precious man of God was ministering, and the Holy Spirit was so thick it was all he could do to speak through his tears. As we were in worship and adoration to our Jesus, I began to burn in my left lung. As soon as that happened, the minister said, "There is someone here with a lung condition, I'm not sure if it's one lung or both . . ." I couldn't hear what he said next. It was like the moment was so important to soak in, my hearing went out. The burning had moved to my right lung, too, so both were now burning. My sister-in-law was pushing me up to stand, and I was pulled to the front into the arms of the sweet Sister Margret. (Fun Fact: Sister Margret is of a darker skin complexion than I, and when her, her husband, and a member of her church came to visit me in my hospital room for the first time, they were praying down heaven so hard, a nurse took notice and it blessed her. You can have church anywhere!) The burning lasted for what had to be ten minutes, and then my lungs went back to normal. Of course, I was in awe and trying to think on how amazing it felt and training my mind to believe something was *done* no matter what it feels like.

We went back to the hotel, and I got ready to do my nightly nebulized medications, including one of the heavy-duty ones. I would be twenty-one days off it and then back on, alternating between two drugs. This one, which I was about fourteen days into, had a few serious side effects, including loss of hearing. Granted, that's for patients who stay on it a long time, and the doctors don't think much about that because CF doesn't promise a long life. But I had already had major ringing in my ears after only a few months of taking it. The doctors didn't understand why that was happening, and I was also getting really dizzy. After this experience, I thought about what God had just done. I told Jack all about what I had felt, all while trying to talk myself into believing I was touched even though my lungs still felt the same. He asked me, "Were you healed?" I paused and soaked in his question as faith and reality circled in my head. "I believe I am healed, yes," I said back. "What are you going to do about it?" he asked. I made a big decision right then, one Jack didn't even see coming. I decided to stand on faith alone. I stopped everything. No more medications, no more nebulizers or pills, not even an inhaler. I was going to place my life completely in God's hands. After all, didn't God say doctors and medication wouldn't fix me? That only He could? Seems like a pretty clear statement. Didn't God also say He would reverse it? Didn't He say in my mother's dream that He would be the one to heal me?

So many reasons to just trust Him and walk on faith.

Now the natural side to this. The medications were not stopping Cystic Fibrosis; they weren't even stopping the fast decline like they were supposed to. I was constantly up and down even when doing all they told me to. They had to tell me to my face, "Don't worry about the negative side effects of this medication because it will be years and years before you will experience any." But I want to live years and years, so tell me what this medication is going to hurt later on so I can decide if a temporary fix is worth that long-term destruction. That last hospital stay was in my mind—an absolute whirlwind of bad news of a fast decline. I get it, the doctors can only look at *now* because CF isn't merciful, and it takes you out before many would consider it to be "your time to go." The medications only promise to slow down the progression of this disease, and for many patients, that's enough. That's all the hope they have. But me—I had my whole life ahead. I had never been this sick before and that's with all these meds. So, here goes everything. Another crutch gone—medication!

My body didn't suddenly feel better; in fact, I was in much pain. The day after I made this choice, Jack and I took a day to go enjoy Tennessee, and I felt so strong in my body! I was able to actually enjoy time with my husband. But I made another promise to God that no matter how bad it felt at times, I would not step backwards. If He wanted me to take something or go to the hospital, He would have to really tell me to. My faith was sky-high at this point. I went to National Arts Festival, which was in Houston, Texas, and boy, was I packing light. No nebulizer or medicine bag like usual. I was completely unafraid and not slowing down at all, despite the pain. Now came the fun part: my clinic visit. I wasn't going to hide anything or sugarcoat it; it was time to lay it all out for them. It felt like I was walking into the lion's den. I'm not going to lie to you; I was scared. The normal flow of my visit goes: vitals, weight, PFT, then the dietitian comes in followed by a social worker, and then one of the two main doctors. I was hoping for the one who is more chill and happier and not the one who is a little harder on me and often suggests hospital stays.

So, they did vitals. My oxygen was low and heart rate was way up because I was nervous. Weight was down a few numbers and same with the PFTs. So, this was going great so far (NOT). I was dreading having to tell each member of my team one-by-one about me stopping all my treatments; I just wanted to get it over with. As I was expecting my dietitian, my main doctor came in, and not the pleasant one I was hoping for. But he was oddly in a great mood. "Your numbers are down a little, what's going on, talk to me." I answered him with, "I have lots to tell you, can we get the whole team in here, so I don't have to say it over and over?" He looked puzzled but said, "Sure! Oh, what medications are you currently on, real quick?" I looked at him and said, "That's what I want to talk to you about." All my team wears gowns, gloves, and masks, so all I have to read are his eyes, and they grew very concerned and confused. "Bethany, what's going on?" he asked. With a deep breath, I took him all the way through my story. I told him about all the confirmations God had given me and that this was what I was supposed to do. I assured him this was not a decision just made on a whim but that my whole life had led to this step of faith. I told him how much I love and respect the CF team and am so thankful for them taking care of me in the only way they knew how. I cried with every word and tried to make a very long, intense, detailed story short. "I will come in here one day over 130 lb., breathing with new lungs, with a baby in my arms." That's how I ended my explanation. My doctors—another crutch gone.

During this time of pure faith in my life, I began to search my life and do anything and everything to ensure my healing. I felt like I had to keep proving myself worthy of it. I struggled with feeling worthy of such a miracle. I still cared what people thought of me way too much. This was when Jack helped me more than anyone. He does not care what anyone says or thinks about him. Sometimes it can be annoying just how much he doesn't care. But I admire that trait in him. When he worships in church, he sings so loud and carefree that people often move from in front of him. I would get embarrassed, but I wanted to be so free like that. I have always looked up to the way my mother could talk about God to anyone, anywhere, without fear of what they would think. I started to think, "How can God trust me with this giant miracle if I am so worried about what people think? If I care too much, I'm not going to share my story with anyone because I won't want to be rejected."

At this point, I was dealing with all my flaws by facing them head-on. I wanted to do something out-of-the-norm for me. I had always danced as I did as a child in my living room, which was my most intimate form of worship, and it had been told to me through prophecy that Jesus loves it when I dance. So, I thought maybe I had to get over what other people might say and dance like I do at home out in public. I was uncomfortable at the thought of bringing something so intimate to a public setting, but I was determined to get my healing and was willing to try everything. So, I had already built it up in my mind. I was about to dance at the altar during a church service. I was walking up to dance, and my heart was racing. As soon as I got to the front, the song ended. In the silence, a wave of His presence hit me, and I began to weep. That was all I could do; I fell to my knees and a woman came up to me and said in my ear, "The Lord wants me to tell you to REST. Rest in His presence."

After that, many more people told me the same, "Rest." So I stopped trying to impress or prove something to God and just waited on Him and fully trusted His process. Uncle Scott told me in a word during this time, "Ninety days from when you stopped your treatments is when the restoration process will begin. When you took that step of faith, you began your march around Jericho. In ninety days you will shout, and the walls will crumble and everything the enemy has stolen from you will be released and given back to you." This word gave me such hope. Everything the enemy has stolen . . . it will be mine.

Restoration Begins

During this time, my father had been experiencing God's touch in his own life. He had gone through another one of his breakdowns earlier in 2018 and lost his job in the middle of it. This was the first time we walked through this without our mother helping us. Thankfully, family paid the rent for them for the months he was unable to function enough to work. Tearsa had to care for both of our parents, and I had to help at a distance because the emotional distress was causing me to get sick and weak. I had to lift them up only through prayer and be there for my sister as much as I could from afar, which hurt me to the core. Much was going through my mind on how to help her. I asked her if I needed to place them in assisted living facilities or try to get their family members to take them. She refused all that because they would be separated from each other and from her. She took care of them both for months on her own.

My sister is a warrior herself. She has had to face losing each of us and yet remains a rock. I can't tell you with words how strong she is; I am so honored to call her my sister. That little sister I asked God for was now carrying it all on her own with only God's help. I hated the thought of her carrying this alone. During this time, my father went through so much mental torture from the devil. All of his past guilt, mistakes, and failures were being thrown back into his face, and he would dwell on these things. Such a dark, dark place he was in. You could see it in his face and in his eyes. All of life's regrets piled up and crushing him as he struggled to wake up each day just to have another day of torment.

The devil threw everything at him, saying that the reason I wasn't being healed was because of his sins, and that my mother was the way she was because of his sins. It got so bad that he almost ended his life (which none of us knew about until he told us later). Eventually, months later, he started to fight back. He said he was looking at Tearsa on the couch sleeping and said to himself, "I have to fight for her. She doesn't deserve this." That revelation given to him by God Himself gave him the strength to climb out of the pit he was in. He came back to us and went looking for work. He got a "gig" (as he calls it) in Orlando running sound for a Christian conference called the "Live to Love tour." He thought this was a great first job.

God moved for him there! He was told by God, "I'm fixin' to show off in your family." We stand on that word as a family. We have been through so much as a family, all kinds of battles: mental, physical, emotional, and spiritual. We are more than ready for the Victory!

I was at a place where my respect for my dad was there, because I would always respect him, but my love was almost gone. I was angry at him for never being the spiritual leader he needed to be, and so my mom had to be. I blamed him for many things.

I was on the phone with an aunt of mine who is a minister, and she was praying with me about my healing. As she was praying, she said I needed to forgive my father. I instantly felt heat all over me, and I agreed to repeat after her as she led me in a powerful prayer of forgiveness, and in my heart, I forgave him. I felt a breakthrough happen, and I just began to pray for him, though not as much as I should have. I told him I loved him and forgave him for everything.

He began going back to church and began changing his life with a passion like I had never seen him have before. I went over to their house, and I remember him asking me if he could pray over me. He started praying, and .I felt it. I felt the power behind his words. Our relationship was completely restored. I believe he was the first thing given back to me that the devil had stolen. (Author's Addition: I used to look at my father's battles through a selfish filter, so focused on how it affected me. I have learned that as God's children, He loves us enough to stop us when we are heading for a path that leads to destruction. Hebrews 12:3-11 makes you change your whole way of thinking. You see how much He loves you, to correct you so you don't continue to be separated from Him because of your sin, and you also have a healthy fear towards Him, knowing Papa's going to get you if you act out of line, just like a good earthly father does. As His child, you need to respect and honor Him by keeping His commandments. I love what 1 John 5:3 says; He doesn't want His commandments to be a burden; we should delight in obeying Him. We should strive to make Him proud of us! I don't know about you, but this gives me a new perspective on facing trials. We are absolutely affected by our loved ones' chastening, but rather than whine to God and beg Him to make *your* pain stop, realize this isn't about you. It might be a lesson from Heavenly Daddy to save their soul. Pray for them!)

The relationship I have now with my father is a treasure to me. I have seen him love my mother the way God loves her for the first time in their marriage. I've seen his prayers move the hand of God in my own life. I am so thankful to have him by my side, supporting my step of faith. I went to church one Sunday evening, and it was a super special night for me as I proudly walked in with my father and sister. While I was worshiping, I looked next to me, and he was worshiping the exact same way. I never knew that we worshiped the same unique way. I was brought to tears. We have had so many moments at the altar, so many texts to each other full of encouragement, and many tears together. We now trust God together to restore my mother back to perfect health. We all miss her so deeply, but we see her smile more each day. Her spirit is very much what it always has been.

Since my father has taken up the mantle of spiritual head of the home, I believe that weight has been lifted from my mother's shoulders. When I visit her, she will laugh with us as we remember funny life stories and she prays with me every night. I had the most precious moment with her. I was struggling to breathe, and it was just her and me at the house. I was in tears, and she came and sat beside me in her timid way, as she picked at her fingernails like she does so often. She looked so worried for me, and she started to pat my back with the little bit of strength she could muster up. I told her I was okay and that she didn't have to pat me. She stood up in front of me, and she started to sing, "I love You, Lord. And I lift my voice. To worship you, oh, my soul, rejoice . . ." I was sitting on the couch just looking up at her through my tears. She held my face with her hands and instructed me with tears in her eyes and a big smile on her face, "Sing Bunny." So I did. Through the pain, I sang with my mommy as she lifted her hands to Heaven, praising. We sang for an hour. The Lord was in the room with us; I'm sure of it. I began to feel strengthened. Restoration is coming. I know it!

God will also restore joy where there have been many tears in my marriage. This has been a step of faith for us both! At the beginning, we both were so strong, but the grueling process has become evident on my body and in our spirits. We both pray for a complete miracle, but we also know that God wants us to totally trust Him, knowing that death is not the end. Jack and I want more than having to constantly wipe the tears from each other's faces. I want to enjoy this life with him. He has held my hand through this whole journey, supported every choice and has been the only one to see and hold the Bethany who screams from the pain and punches her pillow out of frustration.

We have walked through these trials and battles holding each other's and Jesus' hands. He asks me how much more I feel my body can handle, and I'm very transparent with him: I feel like this is the midnight hour. Each day is a gift. For a season, I embraced the thought of death, just in case that was the way my healing would come. I wrote my funeral speech to be read aloud, asking everyone not to look at my death as CF winning but as the way God would get the utmost glory. Somehow it would all be okay, and my story would continue through this book and my loved ones. We began to talk about the "What Ifs" after I am gone. I wanted him to marry and have children of his own. Conversations people our age shouldn't have to have.

Eventually, all the talks and preparations made me okay with the idea. After all, He will heal me or take me. Now I was ready for either. Things became grim, and death became more of what I looked forward to because the idea of finally being without pain was what I wanted more than anything. But this wasn't who I was. I was someone who always believed that healing was mine. I saw myself healed and never ever dying from Cystic Fibrosis. As I fought to bring the spirit of life back into my spirit, I was prayed for over the phone by a minister my father was close to. In the middle of praying for healing, he said, "I speak against the spirit of death in Jesus' name." I instantly felt that heat again like I often feel when God does something.

Jack often asks me how I am feeling, and he knows when I am trying to be strong in front of him and not honest. We look to God for strength in all areas: mentally, emotionally, spiritually, and, of course, physically. The waiting is hard. He sees me look a little worse every day, and I know it's beyond hard for a man to watch the one he loves suffer and not be able to fix it. Men love to fix things. It takes a special kind of love to hold your wife as she is doubled over in pain and only be able to pray for God's intervention. He hates to see me hurting and suffering and often cries right with me. Together we fought this hopeless season. After ninety days, nothing felt different, but the process was only beginning, remember?

So, here we are now, June 3, 2019. I have stayed true to my promise and have not done a single treatment or seen any Cystic Fibrosis doctors. I have felt this body become weaker and weaker, but I have seen my fear decrease and my faith grow to a level I never could have imagined. As I am typing this, I am crying, and I'm hurting. I weigh 84 lb. and my oxygen is in the 80s. Just yesterday, I couldn't breathe enough to walk through the store with my father, and today, my husband held me in bed as I just laid there, trying to see his face through my tears, because I just don't know how this is going to go. I don't have an ending to this book, but that's okay. This book is for you to see how I got here. How faith became bigger than fear. How I was able to speak life in the face of death, no matter what report I received. No matter what your body feels, don't stop believing it's healed. No matter how confusing the journey, hold onto your promises and the Word of God, because if He spoke it, He will do it.

I don't know if this is the end for me or the beginning, but I do know my story isn't about giving up . . . it's about giving in.

My story continues . . .

...And Continues

Man, that ending was so poetically perfect, I couldn't mess it up. I mean that was T-shirt worthy stuff. I know, you thought that was the end of the book. What happened was . . . in the process of getting the book ready for the editor, so much happened! I had to write this alternate ending. An extended edition. Whatever you want to call it. It will be arranged like diary entries, so you have a timeline.

July 4, 2019

Went to Campmeeting again with Jack and his family in Cleveland, Tennessee, you remember the one. I knew God was going to show up in a big way, and I was in expectation. He worked it out for the exact same minister to be there on the exact same night. So, on the one-year anniversary, the minister asked my father-in-law about my story, which he had seen in the magazine which that ministry puts out monthly. As he was telling him, the minister placed his hand on the side of my face and said, "One year and the Lord has kept you because you stood upon the Word." As my father-in-law continued, without warning, the minister laid hands on me, and I went down so fast that I almost wasn't caught. He said, "You will go! When the anointing comes, I have to move. There will be a presence of the Lord to transform that little body. If He started it a year ago, He can keep it going another year." It was refreshing. On that trip, I was able to give my testimony at the very pulpit I had always been so blessed from by the ministers who stood there. I was also given the chance to speak at a few other ministries. Each time, I was nervous, but each time, boldness grew inside of me, and many were touched! It was so exciting to share just a part of my story and see how it encouraged others, not to turn away from medication, but to trust God more than medication. You do this by bringing your need for healing to Him daily and asking Him for wisdom, then listening for His direction. If you don't get a clear word, don't stop praying. If you feel led to seek physical help such as medication, pray that your doctor has wisdom and prescribes exactly what you need. Once you get it, pray over the medication that it does exactly what it needs to do, and you experience no negative side effects. Keep Him front and center! It's so worth it, and you will have peace, I promise you. He is peace!

August 1, 2019

Arts Festival was in full swing. We were in Orlando for national competition. I was very weak and unable to walk the miles we had to each day. I was blessed with not only a wheelchair but an oxygen tank just to help with the strain the festival takes on me. Our human video large we coached was called *The Transfer* (which you can watch on my YouTube channel), and it was the story of the woman with the issue of blood. Our team consisted of ten students who have almost all known me their whole lives; one was injured and unable to perform, so that's why there are only nine in the video. I've watched them grow up in my church and had coached them before. But this time, it was different. The story was so relevant to where I was currently. My life had often been compared to hers in prophecy, because she was made whole by faith. I had written a voice-over to begin the human video, and it was spoken as if it were the woman with the issue of blood. The neat part was, from top to bottom it was her speaking, but from bottom to top, it was Jesus speaking.

When writing it, I wasn't thinking of my story at all, only hers. The Bible says she spent all her money on physicians and didn't get better; in fact, she got worse! No hope in the physical realm. The more I looked into the story of this woman, the more I saw my own desperation to receive my healing just as she had. The human video team had all grown up watching me battle this affliction through the years, and they began to intercede for my healing at practices and throughout the whole season, which began around February and lasted until August. All of our hard work boiled down to three rounds of performances. We always had a special time of prayer before taking the stage because our goal for this piece was to see the sick be healed; for them, it was more personal: they wanted their coach to be healed.

As it came time for the first round, they circled around me and Jack and lifted a battle cry of prayers up for us. I felt heat from my head to my toes, and I knew I had been touched through their prayers. After that, I sat back in the wheelchair I had to be in, with the tube going in my nose with oxygen, and I watched these nine kids give absolutely everything they had for God first and then for Jack and me. I was overwhelmed with emotions, and the anointing was all over them. The voice-over began, and in every word, I saw my story. It went like this:

> It was a time not long ago, when the pain was gone, and all did know.
> A time before uncertainty. A time before they rejected me.
> A time before I fought the lie. This is my fate; I'm meant to die.
> In a time where all was lost, the cure, the way, the final cost.
> My broken body was the price. All within me prepares to die.
> As hope passes through, just believe. With one touch, I felt it leave.

Wow! God gave me each word when I wrote this voiceover. I didn't realize it was me. When there was no pain, everyone knew it; I told them all I had been healed on New Year's Eve. Then I took a step of faith, and things became uncertain, and the doctors rejected me. I went through a season of embracing death as a way to prepare myself and those I loved. I had no crutches! No meds, no doctors, no super strong family faith to rely on . . . all was lost. I was alone with just God to lean on. My body became weaker and weaker. My step of faith caused this. I am dying. But then . . . could it be? Am I at the end of my strength, so now He must carry me? I'm reaching for His garment. Jesus, see me! Now we read it from bottom to top. Jesus says:

With one touch, I felt it leave. As hope passes through, just believe.
All within me prepares to die. My broken body was the price.
It was the cure, the way, the final cost, in a time when all was lost.
This is my fate; I'm meant to die. A time before I fought the lie.
A time before they rejected me. A time before uncertainty.
And all did know when the pain was gone, it was a time not long
ago.

With each round, the story became more alive to my spirit. Jesus tells the woman, "Your faith has made you whole." That's what I'm holding to. I'm reaching for my miracle.

August 14, 2019

Jack and I are in absolute full-time ministry. We work at his father's ministry daily from 8:00 a.m. to 2:30 p.m., then we head over to church for Arts Festival rehearsal, worship team practice, a service as youth leaders, a special event—you get the picture. Because of our heavy involvement, we rarely get vacations. We use our two weeks to go to National Arts Festival and Camp-meeting. "What about summer?" you say. We also run a summer program at our ministry, and this is when we really buckle down on extra practices for national competition. Basically, we get little time for just us. So, with the Disney passes Jack surprised me with for Christmas of 2018, we took four days for ourselves and went to Orlando. While we were still under much stress from life, and I was unable to walk but a few steps at a time, we were determined to have a good vacation. We stayed at a lovely little villa with a full kitchen and everything; it was so nice! However, it was on the second floor, which meant going up a flight of stairs. This often took all my strength, and Jack usually tried to pick me up, but I argued that I needed to do it. Pushing myself is beneficial sometimes.

After I eat, walking becomes even more difficult; just like how your breathing is affected when you absolutely stuff yourself, so is mine by just eating until I'm no longer hungry. I even stop before I am stuffed to try to help my lungs out, but it seems like any amount I eat makes things harder. We had just eaten a nice lunch, and we were heading back to the room to rest before going out to one of the parks. I struggled up the stairs as Jack walked one step at a time beside me, stopping every few just to breathe. I was overwhelmed with emotions each time. How could I be this weak? Unable to climb one flight of stairs. We got into the room and both of us laid down to rest. The room was quiet, and my heavy breathing was almost annoying to me as I wanted to just rest.

In a moment's time, my breathing changed from heavy and hard to calm and relaxed, almost effortless. Right away, with my eyes closed, I said, "What are you doing God? Jack, did you hear the change in my breathing?" He didn't answer. I began to just enjoy the feeling of not having to force each breath. Then with my eyes already closed, I saw another layer of black come over my eyelids. My body began shutting down just like on New Year's Eve. But this time, there was a huge difference; there wasn't the feeling of God's presence. My body was slowly dying, and there was no peaceful feeling to hold onto. All I could do during this terrifying moment was to tell Jesus that I trust Him. "I trust you, Jesus," was what I repeated as my lungs and hearing gave out, and my heart slowed down. However, my mind was going a mile a minute. "WAKE JACK UP, THIS IS IT. GET US TO A HOSPITAL. WE ARE DYING." All of this was going through my mind, but I was speaking through my spirit. I began quoting the 23rd Psalm. "Yea, though I walk through the valley of the shadow of death, I will fear no evil." I wasn't feeling Him, but I was trusting Him completely and had no fear. I fought the voice of fear coming from my flesh and spoke through the faith my spirit had. I began to speak the promises He has given me throughout the years. This experience lasted for what felt like forever, lying in my lifeless body, trusting Jesus that He has me even if I can't feel him. I was very much in my flesh and very much in my spirit. I had a choice. Go with my fearful flesh and wake Jack up and let him hold me as I gasp for air, struggle to stay alive, and maybe die in his arms as he tries to quickly do all he could possibly do to save me, which would most likely mean taking me to a hospital, or I could lay back in the arms of Jesus who has promised me He would never leave me or forsake me, so even if I can't feel Him, I *trust* He is with me, and just let Him hold me through this. That is what I chose, and I'm so happy I did.

Eventually, everything came alive with a deep breath, and I heard my husband's voice call my name. I was flooded with energy and told him the whole story as we went to an outdoor shopping center and I walked around for an hour! I'm not totally certain, but I believe I was being tested. In a moment full of fear, would I still trust God even if I couldn't feel Him? I passed the test if that's what it was. I also had a mini-revelation while we enjoyed ourselves at the park. Jack and I went to a show, and at the very end, the big finale, they stopped everything due to difficulties. It was so disappointing to get through the whole thing and have the big ending withheld from us. We felt left with many questions as to what was supposed to happen instead of the underwhelming finish we "enjoyed." We then moved over to a ride, and the same thing happened. The ride stopped right at the end when the story was supposed to have the "Happily Ever After" moment. Instead, it was an automated apology coming over the intercom asking us to be patient and they will have us exit as soon as possible. Jack said, "It's a shame to give up right at the end." That hit both of us between the eyes. It was as if God was saying, "You're right there at the finale; don't give up now!" We were encouraged and recharged in many ways during this trip.

October 21, 2019

Lately each time I go to church, the topic is healing and miracles, and I know we are in a season of breakthrough at my church. The encouragement comes from every angle. So many of the congregation walk around with my key necklaces on,[2] and I'm overwhelmed by the support they give me. My church is large, but I think almost everyone knows me or knows my story. My pastor even stopped everything and asked the whole church to pray for me and stretch their hands toward me during a service. The atmosphere is perfect for a miracle, and each time they pray for healing, I go right up. I'm no longer embarrassed. I love being at the altars and being surrounded by warriors lifting my name to heaven. It's like I can fall to my knees for a moment and not have to fight but let them lift up my tired arms like they did for Moses in the Bible.

To have a church like that is so special. I have received great advice, counsel, encouragement, and support each time I come, so I try my very best to make it to each service no matter how sick I feel or look. I have been told of visions of me dancing in a sunflower field with Jesus and been told words of prophecy that the Lord has the table prepared in the midst of my enemies; it's set and ready. I've also been told visions of me running through the park chasing my children, and of me being at a healthy and even a little chunky weight. These words fuel my fight! I have been told that God is pleased with me, which I pray He is! To have the God of the universe proud of me—I honestly can't fathom that, but I pray it's true. This is where my spirit is at, but my body? Well, let's just say that almost daily, a new pain is felt. The only way I am still alive is God. My lungs are to the point where they feel so congested that it's like breathing through a coffee straw, and sometimes that becomes clogged and I end up beating my chest to open up an airway for my next breath. I have major headaches which I believe are from not getting the right amount of oxygen through the day, and my veins often protrude out all over my arms, legs, and neck, which cause pain.

Sleeping is hard because I have to sleep on my side for my lungs, but my hips ache so badly because of how skinny I am, and I have no padding. The pain wakes me up and I shift to my other side to help my hip, but that causes the mucus in my lungs that has settled on the side I was lying on to now start moving around and the coughing fits begin. Yes, sleeping is hard to say the least. I miss so much work because I don't sleep well. My body refuses to let me push it to get up and ready and head to a six-hour workday. Thank God, my boss (father-in-law) is so understanding and never makes me feel like an inconvenience. I have felt my body stop working multiple times in the strangest locations: restaurants, public bathrooms, and when shopping in the mall. All places where dying would be uncomfortable. A friend of mine told me that maybe I rarely feel these attacks in the comfort of my home because the idea that "This is it. It must be God taking me home" would be too inviting and I would give up the fight. However, I can say again in total confidence that giving up is not something I even consider. I want to live! I want to have babies! Even if things were comfortable, I don't think I would give up. But I don't know. I am glad that the places it happens don't feel right, and in those moments, I fight off fear with trust. Trust in knowing that my last breath will be taken when God allows it.

---

2   See "The Story Behind the Keys."

In the middle of this pain, big news came to the CF community. A new drug was released, and it was a major breakthrough. It targets the actual source rather than just the symptoms. It's being called a miracle drug, and for the first time, it's available for 90% of the patients due to its long list of qualifying gene mutations. Those who have taken this medication have had an increase of 15% or higher in their lung function and have even stopped coughing. It's so emotional for me to see my CF friends finally be filled with the hope I have been so fortunate to always have. Hope for *life*. Something so tangible that looks so good right now, only available to me if I go back to my clinic, if I go back on all my treatments, and if I go back on my step of faith. I would be lying if I told you that the idea of having a "miracle" now in my hands to help stop all this pain hasn't been a struggle for me. I can't tell you how many people have sent me the link to it and been excited for it to help me. But I can't. The more I consider it, the more upset with myself I become.

This isn't about a quick fix. Even though this process has been so far from quick and having some kind of relief NOW sounds so nice, what I'm waiting for goes beyond what this medication can do. This medication can't restore my body like God can. God's word to me still stands as my directions: "Doctors can't fix you. Medicine can't fix you. Only I can fix you." This new drug might be the CF community's miracle, but it isn't mine. I hope it does wonders for them all and helps them live long lives! However, I took a step of faith, like Peter when he walked on water, and now I'm in the middle of the water. Jesus is before me, the boat is behind me. The boat is solid, it seems safe and it's logical. Jesus is standing on the choppy waters, and that alone is wild, and you don't understand it. I can't tell how far away He is from me, but I have a choice.

I am choosing to keep moving toward Jesus, living this story out with no crutches, simply on a word from God and the trust that He will do all He has said that He would.

Now we end this book for the second time. My story is raw, real and full of things I wish I didn't have to go through, but it is also full of experiences I wish I could go back to. I have heard miracles are instantaneous, but healing is a process. This process has made me the person I am. I am someone who has known God in such a special way, and I feel overwhelmed to be trusted with this story. I don't live this life for myself. It would be way easier and less painful for me to throw up my hands and give up, but there is a bigger goal than just my gain. All of this is for God to receive the GLORY. I have done all I can do and stepped out further than I ever thought I would. I have fought fear with faith and faced the reality of death with a spirit full of life daily. This is no attack from the enemy anymore! Satan doesn't have that kind of power over me to withhold what Jesus paid for on the cross. My miracle is in God's hands. His perfect will and timing. So, with all that being said, knowing my journey has led to this point of total unwavering *trust* and total *surrender* . . .

My story ends.

His story continues . . .

Author's Addition

Much has transpired in my story in the year 2020. In fact, it's been by far the most expedited growth in my walk with God ever. Through the book, you will see the "Author's Addition" inserts. They reflect some afterthoughts of mine after coming through such a "car wash" of change.

I had to go back through my book and edit my story though the new filter I have now. That filter is thanksgiving and victory. I look at my story, not through the eyes of questioning why I've had to go through so much "suffering," but I look at it and see how each battle brought growth and equipped me for the next battle. Most importantly, I see how much God has been there through it all. Life can be seen like a video game, unlocking new levels of faith and trust in my God through the different levels of difficulties. I also feel like God has shown me some "Cheat Codes." If you know gaming at all, you know they can help you avoid some things and make the game easier. Here are some things I want you to know.

I have spent intimate time with God, and in that time, I asked Him to please show me who He is in a way I could understand. Reading the Bible was difficult for me because I felt confused when I tried to read it, which wasn't nearly enough. But when I began to ask God to show me, He began to really show me! One night I woke up and had a word in my spirit, so I searched on my phone, "Scriptures about . . ." (whatever the word was). This happened multiple times. I asked Him to teach me about the Father, Son, and Holy Spirit. The Bible became so alive to me, and I'm being totally serious with you, I love reading it. I am a storyteller, so I love the parables and often read them aloud like a drama script! The people in the Bible were *real* and had emotions like us! Especially the prophets. So many amazing accounts of genuine human feelings are in there. I read these stories and sometimes picture them as movies! Even comedies! I just find it so fascinating that God knows me so well to draw me to stories that I can read through my filter—the drama/storytelling filter.

The Bible says in Matthew 18:3, "Truly I say to you, unless you are converted and become like children, you will not enter the kingdom of heaven." I believe this means you need to trust your Heavenly Father to teach you, provide for you, protect you, defend you, and love and correct you as a child does its natural father. Change the filter through which you look at your story. If you can't see past the hurt and anger, ask Him to show you where He was. However, just like a natural relationship, you need communication! He is so good at being there for you, even if you only talk to Him when you need something. However, if you see you are doing that, it is not good, because you will have a sandy foundation that your house can slip right off of when those waves are coming in fast. You will get knocked down by the tragedy or the struggle, and the waves will keep tossing you and tossing you and making you dizzy while you are trying to get back up. Can you picture this? God is there, and He is never going to leave you, but because you are being tossed around so fast, you can become distracted with the situation and turn to fear more than faith. "Where are you, God?" you might say. He is there like He has always been, but if you would have had a firm rock foundation, the waves might bring some water in your windows, they might mess up the exterior of your house a little, but the good news is you are protected and can trust you are safe. Build a strong relationship with our amazing, fantastic, beautiful God. Every part of Him: Father, Son, and Holy Spirit! Dedicate the day to Him every day and speak life and blessings; what your mouth says matters.

God is the only one who judges and knows the heart, yes, but the Bible tells us in Luke 6:45 (ESV), "For out of the abundance of the heart his mouth speaks." Well, okay, so you can get somewhat of a peek into someone through what they say, right? But Jeremiah 17:9 says, "The heart is more deceitful than all else, and is desperately sick; who can understand it?" Um, yeah, okay, but there is that one scripture about the fruit, right? That's how I can tell about a person, right? John 15:1-17 says that He is the vine, and we are branches, and as we abide in Him, we bear much fruit. It tells us that a branch cannot bear fruit on its own, and He also prunes the branches that don't produce fruit, so they will produce fruit. He wants us to be growing fruit from every single branch! He's like a gardener, and we are just growing and growing under his TLC!

What is fruit? Well, the Bible has a lot of references to fruit, doesn't it? I encourage you to look stuff up and ask God to help you understand the mysteries of the Gospel. We live in a day and age where people love investigations and figuring things out. Do that with the Bible! Have Bible studies with a few really smart people who know the Bible and have a great relationship with God. There is no fully understanding everything; don't even try to or your brain will explode. But the Bible says to seek and find, so go for it, man! It's honestly so much fun, and you begin to see God in a new way and to see life through a new filter. God is so much more than what most people just comfortably see Him as. He is there when we need Him. He is longing for a REALationship with you. Remember, He leaves the ninety-nine for the one (which is amazing because He said He will never leave us or forsake us, so He goes after the *one* while remaining with the ninety-nine also because HE IS THAT COOL).

The new filter He has given me has changed my life. It took time and lots of pressing. The hardest part was retraining my mind with God's help to change the way I used to think to how I should be thinking. I have learned to apply scriptures to my life and act on them. If a negative thought comes, right away I speak it gone in Jesus' name, and I recognize the way it brings me down in my spirit, and I ask God to help me catch that thought even quicker because I don't want to dwell on a negative thought or a negative "What if?" Fear comes with different titles; worry, anxiety, and paranoia are all conditions of fear. Through my story, you can see the many, many situations and trials that fed the fear I *was* bound to. Does fear ever fully leave you? I believe you can live a fear-FREE life, yes, absolutely! But the only way is to have such an intimate relationship with the Heavenly Father, Jesus Christ, and the Holy Spirit, so that when life's unexpected fear-filled moments come full-force at you, you remain standing strong in your knowledge of who He is and all His promises for you. To feel scared is one thing; we are human and we jump when things surprise us, right? (Fun Fact: I was watching a movie one time and there was a "surprise jump scare" moment, and I legit upper cut my own chin. I was that surprised and that uncoordinated also. The poor lady beside me was so concerned, and my husband on the other side was very perplexed. Good times.) But to be scared for a moment is different from having fear! Fear is when you allow it to remain in your thoughts. Take fear captive in your thoughts. The next important cheat code is when you catch it in your head, you stop the words of fear from coming out of your mouth. This can stop so many things from coming to be in your life. People who have genetic illnesses or ailments in their lives often say things like, "Well, my grandmama and grandpapa had it, so I have it." Oh man. For real? Do you want to have it? Life and death are in the power of your tongue! Watch what you say carefully! At first you will catch everything, and it's a huge realization of just how many foul curses you actually are speaking. What about things you speak over your family? Start catching those seeds before they spit out of your mouth. Picture your mind like a seed-making factory, and your mouth being the shipping company. Now the great part is you have the choice to sign for the package before you get it. Signature is REQUIRED. People have no authority over the blood of Jesus you speak over yourself and your family! When a curse is spoken over you, you have the choice of taking in that delivered seed and planting it in your little garden and watering it, getting it some good sunlight, thinking on it, dwelling on it, telling others about it, expecting it to take root and bloom any day now, *or* you can give that seed a YEET as the kids these days would say—meaning, send it gone, man! Don't allow it in your Garden of Life. This is so important. If you can control what seeds you are planting, and what seeds others are able to plant, you *will* see a change. Mix this with the intimate relationship with the one who made the Garden, and man, oh man, you're on a roll! I love the growth I have seen in me. How's my health you ask? You know, I'm getting better every day. The change of filter helps body, soul, and spirit. I have more joy now through the hard times. The joy of the Lord is my strength. It's amazing. You should try it. Come on . . . I dare ya! Taste and see, seek and find, knock and watch Him open the door. He really is the BEST THAT EVER WAS AND EVER WILL BE!

And now . . .

I am ending this book—finally, but He continues to write my story. I give Him complete rights to it. He is my author and my finisher. This isn't a one-woman show; it's *our* story. I pray you see the Author's fingerprints on every page of your story like I do on mine.

. . . to be continued.

PLOT TWIST

promise this is the last time I'm going to do this to you. This is becoming a never-ending story. To be frank, I just won't die. But now, you get the plot twist of the century in this *final* ending. I promise...

December 2019

Jack and his family went on a trip to the funeral of a close family friend. I had no strength. I was only rolling out of bed to walk to the bathroom, then back to bed. Then rolling out to walk from the bedroom to the kitchen, and having to stop and catch my breath along the way. Still praying for my miracle but weaker than ever, no fight left in my body yet so much in my spirit, which continuously reassured me that this wasn't the end for me. Jack asked me if I wanted to take the trip with them, and I just felt I couldn't. He asked me to stay with my family since he was scared to be so far away with no way to rush home if I needed him, which he periodically had to do. I felt strongly in my heart that I needed to be alone. Just me and Jesus. If I die, that's how I would rather it be. Sounds morbid, but I went from wanting to be surrounded by loved ones and being held in Jack's arms when I took my last breath to wanting it to just be me and Jesus. I did not want Jack to deal emotionally with seeing it. I've been alone in His presence before and that's the closest thing to Heaven for me. Jack told me to call his cousin, who didn't live far away, if I felt I needed someone fast. To ease his mind, I told him I would, but I was planning on fighting this with no help but God's and had made up my mind that I wouldn't call anyone no matter what. Since Jack would normally work through the day then go to the gym, the day alone was pretty normal. But that night alone was tough. I had my normal bouts of having to shoot up from lying down and gasp for just a little air, then cry out to God for help. I began to worship and sing with the little breath I had, because I love just pushing that limit. A song about surrender came on. Then another. I began to tell God that I surrender everything. I have done this before on my timing, but this felt as if God was prompting me at that moment to give it all to Him. As I did, I felt these words in my spirit: "It wasn't supposed to get this bad." I believed Him, of course, but had no idea what could have been avoided or what moves I could have made differently. I had felt that all I had done was by His direction. So I took it to heart and told Jack when he returned home. He also didn't understand, but it helped us both to see God as merciful in our situation. We both knew that, but it helped to hear that word. I would later understand this word on an entirely clear level.

January 2020

I always looked forward to New Year's Eve for a touch, sign, word, or anything from God, since that was the night He gave me that amazing encounter. Nothing came of this one except for major disappointment. Jack and I were at the last stretch in this run. He would say that something has to happen, and soon. We were both done. Done crying, numb almost. He would ask me over and over how I felt throughout the day. I would talk through what to do with this book when I was gone. I wasn't planning on living long enough to even see it released. I prepared for this to be my last New Year's Eve. Begging God for something, but getting nothing. We got nothing. I began to feel the walls closing in on me. I wanted nothing more than to be free of this pain, and to set Jack free from this pain. But I just couldn't *ask* God to take me. I promised so many people I would never give up. I prepared to die, I even wanted to die, but I couldn't ask or let those watching me know. One day, Jack held me on the bed as we both cried and he told me that maybe I was suffering so much because I still felt like I had the power to choose when I was going to leave. Saying "Take me" felt as if I was pulling the trigger. I was scared to do it. This was becoming a living nightmare. Dreading the pain the next day held, scared of death, all while still not feeling a release in my spirit that it was time. My flesh was preparing while my spirit was believing. Such a terrible middle to attempt to survive in.

February 2020

I went to work each day I could, which wasn't often. I hated the students seeing me so sick, but I smiled for them through it all. They helped me because kids see your pain but don't let you wallow in it; they are going to bring their problems to you and expect you to listen and show your concern for their needs. I loved that—it got my mind off of my own struggles. They would hug me, cry for me, and ask me a hundred times if I'm going to be okay. I promised them I would see them graduate. I couldn't believe I said that, but it just came out of my mouth with such certainty. I promised that I would always be there for them. I couldn't let them know I wanted to die at times, that I wanted to end this suffering. It was like having so many children of my own all looking up to me and needing me and caring about them too much to let them down in such a terrible way. It was a terrible reality that I would one day not be there to tell them good morning, to tell them they were special, or pray with them when they were crying.

During this time God gave me a beautiful worship song. The words just flowed out of my mouth onto the paper. This is one of many He would give. The words are powerful and became my anthem and many students sang it with me. In a chapel service, Tearsa came and we had a special guest minister there. I got to sing my song during worship, but I was shaking and crying because I became so overwhelmed with what I can only think was the anointing and the presence of the Lord. I was both amazed and embarrassed. Some of the students cried as they looked at me; others were just observing, not understanding what was happening. I began to look into all of their faces in what felt like the last time I would see them. I was flooded with emotion. Tearsa was sitting close to the front and I began to hand her the mic to finish the song. She has the gift of singing and it's been spoken over her that her voice will pierce the darkness. She was hesitant at first, then she came up from her seat and finished the song. At the end of the service, the guest minister spoke over me. My word was very encouraging, as they usually are. He said the Lord was healing me. He said it three times; he said He was healing my digestive system, and when he said that, my legs gave out and I hit the floor. He then said that a parasite had attached itself to me, something diabolical, and the Lord was driving it out. It leaves now! He said weeping may endure for the night, but joy comes in the morning, and the Lord says, "Good morning." I wept and laughed as this word soaked into my weak body, which now had fresh hope! I was still shaking under the anointing and presence of the Lord, looking like an idiot but not caring.

After the service, we went to eat with Jack's family, the guest minister's family, and Tearsa. I began to feel as if I wasn't all there. I wasn't feeling the pain I normally do. I was all smiles, and just in love with Jesus and my life. Even with all the pain, I began to see joy everywhere. As we ate, I looked around the table at the faces I loved so dearly, soaking them all in again as if I wasn't going to see them again. I became emotionally obvious; I looked at the minister who was smiling at me and seemed to be observing my demeanor. He knew I wanted to speak and he said, "I think Bethany wants to say something." I began to say that we can't limit the Holy Spirit. He's not to be contained or controlled. It was super random, but it came out.

I began to address each of the people I loved around the table. With tears in my eyes, I told Jack's family how thankful I was to have been loved and let in the way they let me in. I told his father how incredible it was to have such an amazing man of God fasting for my healing so many times. I told his mother how much I loved her and the way she prayed for me nonstop, hugged me each day, and made me feel like I was hers. His sister, how her amazing smile kept me smiling when I didn't want to. I thanked Tearsa for always taking care of me as we grew up. Then I looked at my Jack, who smiled as his tears fell, and I said, "and thank you for always loving me, even when I was unlovable. You are my greatest gift." It felt like goodbye, yet my spirit was bubbling with the expectation of the miraculous.

We left the restaurant and began to take Tearsa home. I was feeling even more detached from reality at this point, and so began the strangest time of my life. Jack had called his friend and out of nowhere, I started laughing, then he asked me if I was okay and I blew raspberries at him! I quickly covered my mouth and apologized, but it happened again. Each time I covered my mouth out of embarrassment and sheer shock. Jack looked confused and didn't know if he should laugh or be concerned. Tearsa thought it was hilarious. Then I just locked my eyes onto Jack, who was trying to concentrate on the thirty-minute drive to my parents' house. I was smiling with a smirk that I'm sure was alarming and just staring at him. He would look at the road, then back at me. The road, then me. Road, me. It was so weird, but I couldn't move.

When we got to my parents' house, I told him I wanted to visit them. He asked me for how long; I told him I wasn't sure, but I needed to be with them for a while. Tearsa got out and Jack looked at me to follow; then I realized I could not move. Arms, legs, nothing. He kept asking me what was going on, steadily getting more shaken up, worried, and frustrated. I wasn't scared at all; I thought it was so ridiculous it was funny. He came around and carried me into my parents' house, where I began to flop around like a rag doll. Trying to stand, almost like when that minister prayed over me and I looked like a car lot sock puppet.

Jack looked at me in total shock as I flopped around, and my mom, who had been watching since I entered the house, looked at him, very concerned for me as well. This was a first for me. After strange childlike behavior, hiding behind the living room furniture asking Jack to come to find me, almost as if a switch was flipped, I began being very matter-of-fact, mouthing off some smart shots at Jack, mocking him almost. Backing up to leave, he asked me when was I coming home, to which I answered very seriously and at this point right in his face, "Till everyone in this house is free." Then I began to get scared, instantly tearing up, and asked him to please not leave me. He left and I remember feeling as if there were two of me, maybe even more! Brave and scared, mocking yet innocent, like a tornado of madness spinning out of control.

I really thought Jesus was using me to heal my family; it was the only thing that made sense. You have read all about the ways they need a breakthrough and I thought great, this must be it. I'm straight-up Bible meets Twilight Zone. This is where the movie of my life hits the peak and you are sitting on the edge of your seat. We refer to it as "That Friday." It also happened to be Valentine's Day. Yay love! Worst one ever! I called Jack at 3 a.m. and asked him to come get me. I hated leaving Tearsa, who was sort of freaked out about it all. We were so connected during this crazy time and felt safe around each other. I kept telling her I needed to be with Jack and that there are no demons here now (a famous line from a human video from our church). It was like my brain was going and was picking out random memories and applying them to the current situation.

Jack picked me up and took me home and it was a seriously weird car ride! The radio was on and they were speaking of demons and angels and spiritual warfare. It felt like I was high on heaven juice, so I was all excited to listen! He would turn it off and I would turn it back on.

The next few days consisted of the same kind of things—saying things I didn't understand and unable to get proper sleep. Your breathing is naturally shallow during sleep, and since my lungs were already barely breathing, so I would wake up from not breathing or from twitching. Wouldn't be long now. Word began to get out that these were my final moments. My family knew, my church knew, and even my dog would not let me out of her sight. It was happening.

March 2020

I had some incredible moments with God while the reality was fading. I think I was more spirit than flesh. After feeling insane yet as clear-minded as ever,

I felt so scared and called my dad to come and get me from home with Jack; I also felt the need to not be with him when it happened. Notice the pattern: wanting to feel safe, so calling whoever I'm not with to rescue me and give me some kind of security or solution to the way I was feeling. At their house, I was mopey and exhausted, but kept asking my dad lots of questions about the mental battles he had fought because I was going through something new in that realm. Thankfully, he helped me feel a little more normal and safe because I was feeling some of the same things he would feel. I felt I had some kind of map and a guide now; he also provided some warnings and triggers.

When I got to their house, I wanted to be with my mommy. I asked her if I could lay down with her in her room, which is a sacred place to her and no one had been in there more than just to clean up for her if she needed us. But she opened her covers and I laid in there with her. I felt peace and safety—exactly what I had been looking for. I wanted to be safe. It was finally time to give up.

Once my mom fell asleep, I didn't think about it long, and I said, "Take me." I closed my eyes and waited. Nothing happened, so I said it again. I wasn't asking at all; I was telling God I was done. Hello? I'm cashing in the card! You said if it hurts too bad, You'll take me, so here I am! TAKE ME! Nothing again. A wave of fear came over me. It was like the worst reality shock, as I now understood that the ticket to heaven I *thought* I had didn't work at all. This means I'm trapped. I'm stuck in this broken body with no escape! I had both fear and peace come over me. I had done all I could do. I passed out asleep from the mental, emotional, and physical exhaustion. It felt great because I had gotten very little sleep for months.

I woke up to a lovely panic attack. My cousin saw my social media post asking for prayer and she asked if I needed her. I told her I needed her to take me to the hospital. She rushed to be with me and called an ambulance. Tearsa was there and got ready with Kasey to follow behind the ambulance, knowing this gave me some comfort. My mom didn't understand what was happening, but begged me to not leave. When they got there, I asked mom to go with me to the hospital to get help too. She shook her head no, but as I was leaving the house, walking toward the EMTs and their stretcher, I asked them to please get my mother and help her. She was scared and closed the door quickly. They asked if the call was for her or me. I said me, and they said that I was who they were there to help, and they placed me on the stretcher. I kept looking at the door, crying and praying that she would come too.

Everything was surreal, spinning out of my control as it had been the past week now. I was feeling like maybe I was going to get the help I needed, even though I was pretty certain it was too late. They began to check my vitals, and they said they were normal. I told them they can't be normal; I am a Cystic Fibrosis patient who has been off my treatments for two years. They calmed me down and continued to reassure me that I was going to be okay. I realized I didn't see my cousin following me and felt alone. We arrived and I was asked the normal information questions, the answers to many of which could not be found in the mess of my brain. I only knew Jack's number by heart and told them he was my husband. I began nearly begging them to please contact him for me. He didn't know where I was. They repeatedly told me to calm down and I was told no beds were available, so I was placed in a chair right in the center of the craziness of an emergency room. I sat there, scared out of my mind, sobbing, alone, and realized that I didn't even have my phone to call anyone. At this moment, fear was like a heavy weighted blanket thrown over me.

I looked around at all the chaos. Screams of patients in pain and rushing doctors. I was curled up on the seat, then, feeling scared again, I walked back over to the desk to ask for them to call my husband for the second time. They walked me back to my seat. Then almost like yelling in my head, I was being told to ask them to kill me. "Someone kill me." Over and over. Even though I was not all there, I knew if I yelled that out, I would quickly be on my way to another kind of hospital. It became almost defining; I could hear nothing else and those words were right on my lips. I squeezed my eyes closed and started praying, begging God to come to save me. I was bombarded with the fact that what I thought was my escape plan had completely failed! It was like the devil himself was right in my ear, teasing me and saying things like, "If that wasn't God you heard, what else wasn't God?" It made me question everything I felt He had said throughout my whole life—if I had heard Him tell me to stop my medication! Was I this sick because I had made this choice to kill my body slowly? These thoughts were as loud as a yell in my ear! I felt dizzy because I was spinning out of control. I prayed in my head and out loud, and in a few moments, I felt and heard peace. No profound word from God, but just His peace, which said everything.

They got me a bed and I began to notice just how critical these people were all around me. Fear waves came and I thought that because I had felt crazy the past few weeks, they had taken me to a mental hospital instead.

The nurse came to me and began to ask me questions, like whether I was hurting myself. I knew enough to understand that if I told her what was going on in my head, she would have had to act on it, and that was a very real concern for me. Both my parents have battled mental illness, and this could be my fight now. I began to keep quiet to avoid saying the wrong thing. When she left, the mental torment began again. This time I saw myself in a padded room with no one I love with me. The feeling of abandonment was so thick I was almost crushed by its weight. I curled up under the covers and wept as quietly as I possibly could. Then I heard, "Curse God and die." This was a new escape plan, which was being played on repeat. I love God with all I am; I would never get to a place where I was so angry that I cursed Him. As much as I wanted out of this dark, life-sucking cycle I was trapped in, it was not enough to turn my back on the One who gave me hope through it all. I refused to say it; it grew louder, a yell. Again, I refused. I felt as soon as the words left my mouth I would die and be separated from God forever. I fought it with prayers and pleas to God again. Finally, silence.

At this exact moment, my sister came to my bedside and held me and I cried and held her too, feeling some sense of security. She told me only one person can be with me and that Jack was there in the waiting room. She asked me if I would rather have him there, and I had a moment where I was scared to let her out of my sight. But I told her I needed Jack. She left and a few seconds later there came Jack. I was safe holding his hand like he always had done in scary situations. I couldn't stop looking at him and soaked in the feeling of safety he gave me. He spoke to all the doctors who came in for me and did what he always did, asking questions to find out what needed to be done. They said my X-ray showed signs of concern and they wanted to admit me and contact my CF team and begin treatments again. I cried and told Jack no, I wasn't going back on them. He asked if there was a way to get me some sleep aid so I could finally rest. They explained that my condition was too bad and that sleep aid would be very dangerous. So we had a choice to make: sleep there or sleep at home. No help from them if I won't take anything, so we left. At home, I took some sleep aid even though I was scared because of what they had said. Jack held me in bed as I twitched and turned, shot up and cried a bit, then finally went to sleep. I began to finally recover.

March 2020

Weeks have gone by. Each day I even slightly felt I could, I got myself up and ready for work. What little strength I have, I never let go to waste. Each time I come through the doors, my students all hug me and tell me how much they missed and love me. Their smiles were like pain killers and a goal to reach each day. We had an incredible chapel service in which one of my students who had recently been enrolled hugged me, looked me in the face, and said, "Your chains are gone now. You are free." My eyes filled with tears and I asked him why he said that. He said God told him to. I couldn't help but smile; if I ever needed a breakthrough and freedom, it was now. At the end of the service, I got the worst news of my life. Jack had been arrested.

Everything was spinning again as I tried to understand. Not even a hug or a kiss goodbye; I was just told he had got a call from the sheriff and he turned himself in. The shock you feel and the questions you have are what I and everyone else who knew Jack felt and asked. The accusations, which took a few days to get to me, were devastating. I didn't believe it. Not Jack. I maintained my composure in public as I went to work and to church—being picked up and given rides for all of it. When I would walk into my empty home, the heaviness of reality would slam me to the ground. There were many days I couldn't peel myself off the floor—I just laid there, confused and alone. I had to make myself eat at least one meal. Sleeping was cold and scary. I felt lost. How could this have happened?

Each little bit of information came from his family to me. It was all I had, and it was never much as they didn't have much either. Word began to spread around our small town, our friend groups, and eventually our church. It felt like everyone knew more than me and I was alone in the dark. Everywhere I went I would get looks that said, "I'm so sorry." This was the new normal. It was like trying to figure out a puzzle with no picture on the box. My mind began searching files and grasping for any form of a clue I could find.

His bond hearing came, and because of the pandemic it was done by phone interview. His family and I listened and asked some questions. The bond was not going to be lowered, and it was completely undoable. Jack checked in on me through his family. He was told my weight, which was at an all-time low of 71 lb. I was weaker than ever, physically, mentally, and now emotionally, sick and still near death. The little bit of recovery I had made since the last ER visit went flying out the window.

One morning I woke up to my phone going off non-stop. His mug shot and the article had hit the local papers: front page in all the main stores and some restaurants. His online article was being shared hundreds of times and he even made the local news on TV. I got both love and support messages and some hate messages. I just set my phone down and got ready for work. No time to cope or process. At this point, I still didn't want to believe it was true and told myself it wasn't. It was just a mistake; he will walk in that front door soon and hold me again! There were days I sat on the floor and looked at the door for hours, just waiting for that moment to come. When these things happen, you are left with only your memories to search and live off of. It was as if Jack had died—there one day, and gone the next. Everyone was reaching out one way or another. Now it was common knowledge. Imagine going to the store to buy your groceries and seeing your husband's mug shot on the front page as you check out, with his crime listed in such a blunt way. My family, especially my dad, would come and be with me as I cried and asked endless questions for which he had no answers. He would let me vent, sob, and whatever else I needed to do as he held me.

Eventually, I got a phone call, and it was Jack. Hearing his voice filled me with hope, and we began to talk every night. We became closer through those calls than ever before. I both hated and loved that. It was the worst feeling to be so confused and not able to ask him to explain and give me answers because I was told not to speak of the case. I was talking to my husband, the man you know from my perspective. He said he would never hurt me. He promised to love me till death. He was a good, faith-filled man! I was torn between the facts coming forward about a criminal, and the love I had for him as my husband. Day after day we grew closer through our calls. Then one special day we got to do a video visit! As soon as it connected, and I saw his face, we both began to cry. Thirty minutes was all we got, which was better than the twenty-minute phone calls, and the whole time a smile never left our faces. I studied my husband through that video visit. The man I loved, the one I was supposed to spend my life with, was now in hand-cuffs and that ugly orange jumper. How did we get here, Jack? Why are they saying you did this? You didn't, I know you couldn't do such a thing! All the things I wanted to say, but didn't. The whole time we cried over the chapter our love story was at. This wasn't in the plans.

Months went by with my marriage being only a phone call for twenty minutes at night, unless he couldn't get out to make one. Those nights were terrible. He had no way to let me know, so I would hold my phone and wait until I knew it was too late for calls. We had video visits three times a week. Often we wrote letters to each other. I loved those because I could hold them and look over them all the time. This was now our relationship.

May 2020

Our eighth anniversary was coming up. We had faith that he would be home for it. I made a chronicle of videos leading up to the day, each one addressed to him in hopes he would feel he missed nothing of this preparation in faith, and soon we would hold each other again and smile, with only these videos to remember this time apart as we celebrated the time together we prayed for! I made a huge wall of memories over the bed for him to see when he got home. All the photos from our honeymoon and the cards we had given each other through the decade of being together! We talked about going back to Tennessee for another honeymoon as soon as he got home. I packed our suitcases and put them in the car, I looked up the cabins we stayed in and nearly booked one in faith, but I waited for him to pick one. Then I waited. We waited.

Our anniversary came and I sat by the door, crying in both expectation and the fear of reality. My father came and ate lunch with me at my favorite local place. It was comforting to have him there with me on the day I had felt such high expectations for Jack to be home, but I would try my hardest to enjoy not being alone, and it would hit me in waves. Daddy would see my eyes fill with tears and reach over and hold my hand as he tried not to cry too, and we would smile. He understood the feeling of being alone very well, since for a few years my mother had not been the same person he married, and we could relate on a good many levels. But he couldn't begin to understand being betrayed by the one you gave your heart to. He could only listen at the times I would grieve and ask him why? I asked him to please take me to the jail out of total desperation to just see him. I convinced myself there could be a slight chance they would let me if I told them what day it was. My daddy, in hopes to bring me some joy, brought me there and we walked into the visitation center. At the desk, I asked them to please let me just see my husband as I held back a flood of emotions. When the answer was given, I wanted so badly to ask again. My father could see it in my eyes, but he thanked them and ushered me out. As I was leaving, I turned and took a deep breath in, soaking in the peace of knowing that Jack was right there. I whispered "I love you" and left. My father stayed with me all day and even took me to a nice steak dinner. When night came, I anticipated our call of course and that was that.

The day was over, but I had been given some new visions which were exciting and gave me more breadcrumbs of hope on such a disappointing day. These new things gave me something to work for now! I had much hope that

Jack would jump right in as soon as we were reunited and help with them too. I would have confirmations left and right about things I would feel in my spirit. Ministers on TV would confirm words; sometimes it would be a word that I was feeling. The day before our anniversary it was "whirlwind." I had a literal experience in my kitchen where I was pouring my tea and began to get very dizzy, then I started spinning, and I had to throw my tea onto the counter and try to stop myself. I was nearly about to pass out from how fast it felt I was going. I latched onto the counter and felt the word drop right then into my spirit. Throughout the day it was confirmed multiple times; God was turning it around, and He would do this so quickly. I took this as more faith power!

I can't properly tell you with words how sad, delusional, and yet hopeful I was. Our whole marriage we had prayed for my miracle; now we prayed for his. This situation was so beyond different and yet I was so blind by denial I applied the same faith. More and more information was coming to the surface and I couldn't talk to Jack about any of it. The calls between us remained as if nothing was changing. I would have looming questions throughout the day, trying to find excuses as to why he couldn't have done this. I went through my entire phone trying to place where he had been at all times. This caused my mental and emotional stress to increase daily. Then I'd suppress it all in faith, sure that none of it was true because it was my Jack. By the time he called, there was no worry; his voice brought the comfort that I was starved of through the day. He felt . . . safe. He spoke with love in his voice and our days felt similar—trapped and alone. We would have encouragement to share that we had collected each day before the calls, and oddly enough, they almost always coincided with one another—sometimes word-for-word. It was as if we were seeing the power of couples when they both become so dependent and desperate for God to move and have zero distractions. This is what could be! A couple so connected to the Father and each other that they feel the same things in their spirits! We would say how much we loved this feeling of connection, and we never wanted to lose it.

One day a detective came to my house and went over evidence with me. I was mostly quiet, then shared how I felt and my unshaken disbelief in everything which didn't go with what I felt. It was like when I would get a bad report from the doctors and would speak the opposite. I applied the same blueprints I had lived by to an entirely different situation. Evidence and people's words didn't change how I felt. I wasn't talking and loving the criminal; I was loving my husband. I wanted nothing more than to wake up and find him right beside me again, and to realize it had all been a lie! Until then, my Bible and his picture laid there on our bed. This would one day be over. During this month I reached 80 lb. and began to cough stuff out of my lungs! There was much growth in me; the Lord told me to dwell in the secret place. So I did, daily, and I loved it! There my body, soul, and spirit became stronger.

July 2020

I began getting excited as I was finally reaching my long-awaited thirtieth birthday! By this time I was 99 lb. Almost to 100! No medications!

Being alone and stuck in my house wasn't too terrible since I wasn't the only one, due to the pandemic. I took the time to seek and talk to God like never before. He was my only comfort. I knew I was alone now and needed to get some things done that seemed impossible, but I knew I couldn't make it alone without driving. I was not going to ask for rides anymore. I began to take what little brain function I had to study for that learner's permit test. This was nearly impossible because I couldn't form thoughts well. How could I remember which way to turn the steering wheel while parked on a hill? I studied for about a week and then went in to take the test. I failed terribly. While I was there trying to concentrate (which was humorous with how short my attention span was), I overheard the DMV lady telling a woman with diabetes that she needed to bring in a doctor's note saying she's able to drive despite her diagnosis. I decided to check if CF needed a doctor's note saying I could drive, and Google took me to a page that said a big ol' YEPPEROO.

While I soaked in this beautiful piece of information, a minister I was listening to said that Jesus isn't walking around doing miracles today; He uses people to bring them. I then saw a small vision of new lungs coming to me, like through surgery, with doctors all around. I immediately called my CF clinic after years of being away. They were surprised to hear me and expressed their excitement for me to come back. I was scheduled for that week! I was super nervous to be told how bad I was, to see on paper and X-rays what I was feeling inside. But I knew this was God's directing, so I was at peace about it. I spoke to Jack that night and he began to pray with me about it!

I went back. I walked in the door looking very different than what I wanted to. I wanted to be healed when they saw me next, but that wasn't the case. They welcomed me with open arms and said how good it was to see me. If I had passed the three-year mark, I would have had to find a different clinic—which means I would have been more than welcome to return anytime the past few years.

They began to do my normal routine CF things. My PFT (lung function) was by far the very worst it's ever been, at 0.73L (close to lung transplant level). Rather than throwing me into the hospital, they understandingly listened to my current life status and started me on the bare minimum treatments. To be alone and secluded in a hospital at this time would have been very hard on my emotional and mental health.

The plan was enzymes, albuterol, and hypertonic saline. Within a few weeks, I had gained about 20 lb. and began to climb in lung function, to my, and my doctor's, surprise. I knew it was my Jesus showing off. I may not have come back the way I wanted to, but I felt He wanted them to watch the reversal of my decline like He had said in a previous word. He would reverse it. Back to this whole CF life cycle—but now, spiritually strong in a whole new way. God had truly sustained me.

August 2020

I had the most incredible moments with God. *All* my crutches had been removed and I was now forced to walk on my injuries and rely on only Jesus for support. Some days were more painful than others, emotionally, mentally, and physically. Alone in my empty house, with just a haunting memory of what was, I found comfort in routine. Wake up, dedicate the day, my heart, and my life to Jesus, then I would read out loud my scriptures and speak life and healing (three times a day). After that I would worship, eat and take communion, study for my driver's license, clean the house (because I felt God tell me to get my house in order), lay out and get some sun, watch some ministers online, time of worship and prayer again, then my phone call with Jack, then pray until I fell asleep. Repeat.

During this time, God put me through a season of training. I obeyed everything I felt he told me. One day it was to make a *huge* pot of chicken noodle soup and give it out for free, with one condition: to pray over the ones who ate it for any needs they may have. Even if I didn't understand why, I would obey. I realized a pattern: when I would obey, Jack would get an answer or a sign of encouragement almost at the exact same time. Like the story where he obeyed and placed his money in the offering bucket and I heard the confirmation that I was praying for. Obedience unlocks confirmation.

September 2020

My next clinic visit was here. I went in and they cheered me on about how well I was doing and then they talked to me about a new medical treatment for CF that was life-changing. In the words of my doctor, "CF is no longer a death sentence." I began to cry when he said those words. Now the hope I had my entire life through faith was tangible. I was told I would be able to have children, to grow old, to *live*! They told me I had the perfect gene mutation to take a groundbreaking "miracle drug." We began paperwork immediately, and what should have taken months to get took only weeks. Soon I had had my gift from Heaven in my hands and took my first dosage. Right as I did, I began to cough up so much stuff! Effortlessly too! It didn't hurt one bit nor was it violent. I know it's nasty, but I coughed up an entire water bottle full. (I wanted to measure it.) I instantly felt better after doing this for only three days. I never coughed violently again! It was truly unbelievable. Lung function climbed in a couple of months and keeps climbing. I would have moments of sheer joy and cry so many happy tears while I laughed out loud. I couldn't remember all that pain I had been in! All those things I couldn't do, I couldn't recall. I can do everything I want to do now! I went and took my driving test and passed right away! Now I'm driving around town, going to work and the grocery store on my own, and able to walk around and carry my bags to the car! I was only missing my Jack. So many things to be thankful for. How could I even be upset? When the waves of loneliness hit, I called on Jesus for comfort. Some nights it felt like He was physically holding me. Literally a brand-new life.

October 2020

Reality began to creep up on me as Jack's case came into the spotlight. The option of a trial or plea was his choice to make, and all I could do was tell him for either one, I'm here, and either way, God will be God. We have no control now. Just faith for a miracle. Jack ended up taking a plea deal, and the wait was unbearable. I wanted him home, the Jack I loved. Now even more connected on a soul level. I still felt hopeful because we had promises that had to be fulfilled! All the words through the years promising us children. It has to be, and now I can have children! Something must happen!

There was a chance the sentence could be lowered at the mediation, where I would go to speak on Jack's behalf. I didn't think twice about it! I wanted him to be with me and nothing else really mattered. He was locked into my memory as the amazing faith-filled man and lover he was to me all those years.

I had by now heard most of the details of his case. Each time something new came to light, it was like taking a knife and stabbing it in my back and twisting it over and over. But I just kept believing and hoping; remember, I'm built tough with this unstoppable faith. So no matter what it looked like or what I was told, I was accustomed to believing in the impossible. He couldn't have done this. I believed him when he said "I love you" each night on our phone calls. He talked about the future with me; he wouldn't do that if he had done this. Each night we planned what we would do as soon as he would get home. With all of this on my mind, I fought for *our* story.

On the day of his mediation my dad, best friend, and Uncle Scott came over beforehand to pray with me. I remember feeling so many emotions: some excitement because he could be coming home with us because none of it was true; some fear of hearing details of this case I didn't know yet; the sinking feeling that he would be in the same room with me after all these months and I couldn't even hug him. Mostly I felt the numbness of reality that we were really in this position where one man can decide Jack's life, and my life.

Uncle Scott said he was praying that morning and he was reminded of when he first held me in his arms. He was stiff and afraid and my mother said, "It's okay, Scott, you're not going to break her." He knew the Lord was telling me that whatever happens, today wasn't going to break me. This was the encouragement I needed.

As we waited in the lobby, my heart was pounding. Then the doors opened, and there he was. I wasn't prepared to see him so quickly through the doors. Just seeing the back of his head took my breath from me. There was my husband, sitting there with a shaved head, orange jumpsuit, and handcuffs, in a posture of shame and defeat. We were made to sit behind him, and he never turned around.

I tightly held my dad's and my best friend's hands to keep calm as the mediation began. They started with the prosecutor, who spoke of the crime in a harsh and straightforward way, which made hearing the things he said even more piercing. The crime involved our marriage, love, and even friendship being completely and utterly betrayed. I didn't want to believe it; word by word I disregarded to keep my heart and mind pure for when I went up to speak, almost instantly forgiving before even feeling the pain. As soon as all the details were spoken, it was my turn. I walked up to the stand, holding his wedding ring in my hand which I had been wearing around my neck since his arrest, and looked over to finally see his face. The mask covered it, but his eyes said it all. I watched him look at me, shocked at how healthy I finally was; no longer bones, no longer holding onto walls to try to walk a few steps, and no coughing. What we had prayed for was now in front of him. Tears filled both of our eyes to the point I could barely read my words. I spoke as clearly as I could as I fought for Jack this one last time. This was not for anyone more than it was for Jack. I wanted him to know who he had left—who he had given up. Someone who forgave and loved all these months because I believed him.

When I finished, I felt the heaviness grow even heavier as time was closing in to the final decision. The others spoke, then his attorney, and finally Jack spoke. He expressed regret and guilt. It was then, hearing him say it . . . I knew he had done this.

He was the criminal they were describing. He did those things they said. The room began to fade and I just felt . . . nothing. It was like watching a loved one pass and give that final breath. The judge spoke and sentenced him to the maximum time according to his plea. When the sentence was announced, it was as if the dam broke that contained all my pain. I let out a wail and held myself in my arms, doubled over from the reality crushing me.

The moment he was out of sight, I collapsed onto the floor. I just looked at the grooves in the carpet, all the little colors you can't see when standing, and they all began to morph together; I couldn't see, hear, or feel anything. I was picked up and carried out of the courthouse and all the way to the car. A part of me had died. Emotionally I was numb. Blank stare. Replaying every word. Every moment. Every expression he had. I fought for him as he fought for me. The situations were entirely different, but to me, I felt as if I had proved my love was real. I fought for my Jack, the one throughout the pages of this book now that Jack was gone. I mourned his death. This was all wrong. I was supposed to be the one to die. He had a whole new life to live without me! I wanted it to be beautiful for him. Now here I was—no vision for the future because I didn't think I needed one, and the only one I had in faith was with Jack! This wasn't supposed to be part of the story.

They began the process of transferring him to prison, and being his spouse, we could have a contact visit, but due to the pandemic, they kept glass between us. I had picked up all his mail and belongings from the front desk, including the clothes he was arrested in. It was a morbid feeling, holding his clothes in a clear trash bag, all untouched from the last time he wore them. They placed us in two rooms separated by a wall of glass. They brought him around the corner and I instantly teared up. He walked into the empty room with an officer and gave me a little smile as she took off his handcuffs. Looking at me with both deep regret, fear, and joy, he walked up to the glass and grabbed the phone, so I did too. We laughed at how I couldn't figure out the right buttons to press and had to read his lips for the instructions. When the moment of laughter ended, I began to soak in his drastically altered appearance. He was always a strong-looking man, physically, mentally, emotionally, and spiritually. I was always the weak one in most of those areas. Now it was as if we had switched places. I looked into his eyes the most because that was the only part of him that I recognized—the only part that was left that felt familiar. He couldn't stop telling me how healthy I looked, asked me to stand back so he could see from my head to my feet; he smiled and cried. It was like we were living out a movie.

Our visit didn't give us much time to have a casual conversation. One of the very first things I told him was that I forgive him, which I could see lifted his spirit and his demeanor changed. He heard my heart, my pain, my regrets, and after all of my words were heard and after his apologies were spoken, I asked him to let me go—but not to let me go. I couldn't fully ask him what I needed because it wasn't what I wanted! Conflicted with my heart and faith and reality yet again. But there was no other choice. He cried a moment, closed his eyes as the tears fell, then opened them, looking right past me, and said he released me and that he supported any choice I made. When he told me this, I physically felt a change—a shifting you could say. We ended our visit with many tears and with our hands against the glass on each other since we were unable to hug goodbye. I said my goodbye with these words: "You chose a path I can't follow. You were my first choice." The visit was over and we hung up the phones. I watched the officer come in to get him and cried almost uncontrollably as she took his hands and placed handcuffs on the hands that used to hold me. It was over for us. Jack left my story. The reality finally took over the faith, and I understood that he had made a choice in which even God had to allow justice. It hurt me, yes. But I eventually understood that people can make choices that can destroy their promises and words of what *could* have been. This is a hard truth of the power of our choices.

Soon my home was sold, my belongings I had no room for were sold, and I had several emotional outbursts in my nearly empty home where my dad would just have to hold me as I screamed. I got a new job and in a matter of weeks, I was back in the house I had left when Jack and I began our story. Back in the exact same room with my sister. Just me, my puggle Belle, and a few boxes from that life. Back to square one. It was time to start over. To heal.

Since I've been home, my father went through another breakdown. This one put him out of work for a while, but I was right there to help him and reassure him that everything will be fine. This time it was different because he was completely doing life right. No sin to feel guilty of to bring on the stress which brought on the breakdown. He struggled to understand why this was happening when he had done nothing wrong, and so we had many conversations with each other about this just being something that we now knew was not a punishment because of his choices, but a need for healing. I held my dad's hand as he processed this and began to try to work through this mental illness in a new way—as an illness in which we were not just relying on faith, but works also! Seeing doctors and getting answers, then doing all we could to get and stay well. He quickly recovered and went back to working. I've really seen how not everything negative in our lives is punishment! Not everything is linked to how good a Christ-follower you are. Bad things happen simply because this is earth and not heaven. God is all things good! He sees your heart behind your actions. Who are we to tell people they are having hardships because they are being punished? People say that. I thought that about my sickness, my father's illness, and sometimes judged other people's trials with this mindset too. But to say that is to say that God gave that punishment to the same people He sent His Son to die for so they would be forgiven for their sins. I believe God is merciful and He is faithful to forgive, so we don't have to be punished! It's all in your heart condition. This was a true life lesson my father's condition taught me. Now we all fight every battle together as a family, like we always have.

The Bryans are tough because life has required it! We could not make it without God.

I told you it was a plot twist.

I have felt things I wished I never had to feel, and I would be lying if I told you I remained my strong, faithful self through it all. There were times I cried and asked God why; why did I have to experience this pain of physical, mental, and now emotional death? I now had the opposite problem I did for nearly all my life; now my body was working and my spirit was dying. Giving up spiritually felt way more deadly. I loved Jesus now more than ever, but the drive for life was leaving, and being with Him in Heaven was my only real desire. Life here felt done. The only thing those all around me could say was "I'm so sorry, Bethany." No one had walked this journey before and could offer help or comfort. Here and there people could relate at some level, but not one person could understand fully. I didn't understand fully. I was so very close to death. Why not let me die before this? I have often been referred to as Job. I always laughed it off, but in a way, my story was all about hardships, loss, and pain. My broken body, my sweet mother becoming someone else, my father leaving us time and time again mentally, now my love Jack was gone, with the most painful exit of my story. How much more would I have to go through? Although all these questions came and went and the waves of emotions followed, I never blamed God. He was the only one I was certain would never leave me.

I was crying out to God one day, saying, "I'M NOT JOB! I DON'T WANT TO BE JOB!" and in almost a loud but soft whisper God said, "Job's story was about Job's faithfulness. Your story is about mine." This has been something I lean on when my flesh takes the driver's seat and my spirit is the backseat driver trying to give direction. I have struggled with the insecurities that come from a spouse's betrayal. Feeling ugly, unworthy of being loved, guilty of being less than I should have been as a wife. I would replay every small argument we ever had to see where I could have been better or said something different. I was in a state of mind where I didn't blame Jack for his choice but blamed myself. I justified him leaving me because, in a weird way, it hurt less. I was broken physically—unable to be the perfect wife I wanted to be. Broken emotionally at times due to the pain I was in. What kind of a life was that? I began to pile up the baggage we once carried together and walked alone with it. I became bitter toward myself, which eventually made me harsh. Words came from my heart of anger and frustration—all while others around me constantly told me it wasn't my fault, without me ever saying I felt it was. There is a letter Jack wrote me from jail that I would read over and over, expressing his love and appreciation of who I was and that I was a good wife and that I of all people didn't deserve this. It was my only reassurance that even if I wasn't perfect, Jack knew I loved him and I was a better wife than I felt I was. I know it's something I can hear a million times and it means nothing if I don't allow my heart to be healed by God. I will get there.

I reached the anger stage of grief, and those closest to me watched and heard me change.

No students watching or listening to me. No parents telling me what to do because I'm an adult. No husband to help sharpen my dull edges and call me out. It was just me.

Church became a now and then occasion, and I left all leadership positions so I could go through this shedding on my own, without those who would be impacted seeing me. I was limping hard without my crutches. The pain of my injury was obvious now, so I hid. With the pandemic and my illness as excuses, I stayed in the shadows without people questioning it.

I went to a service with Uncle Scott and he spoke about God telling him to always be transparent, because when you are, the light goes through you to others; if you are a mirror, the light deflects off of you. When I heard this, God brought my dream back and I saw a part of it in a new way. He showed me how I became transparent and watched my body heal. But I never really saw the transparency as anything more than a window to see the inside being fixed. Now I felt in my spirit that it had a deeper meaning. I feel we are too prideful to admit we are not as strong as we should or could be. I feel when we put on the mask of strength that we have customized to fit and looks just right, we become unrelatable, untouchable, and unable to heal properly.

Let those who are stronger than you help, and those weaker than you see you limp. They should know they are not beneath you, but beside you. This is me, being transparent. I'm hurt and limping, but still trying each day to walk and growing stronger. My body is recovering and my heart is also. I smile more than I cry because I am not where I was.

His timing was perfect when I felt it was too late. It wasn't supposed to get this bad because I couldn't get my miracle when the drug first came out because by then Jack had already sealed his future and God knew that. If I would have started treatments, I could have started the family we prayed for and were promised. This would have been so much harder for me and the children who would have lost their father.

I cried then because children were out of reach, but now I understand. It has taught me a very important lesson to wait, trust, and not get upset when it doesn't happen. He sees the box with the entire picture while I'm only holding a corner piece trying to place it.

Life has a way of teaching you the things you need to learn. You don't know the whole story, only the page you are on. The next chapter holds challenges you can't face without the lessons the last chapter taught you. Breathe in deep and remind yourself, "It's just a page; it's not the whole story."

All of us have a story which has shaped our chapters. None of us can understand each other fully because we are never on the same page, the same book, or even on the same shelf. The only thing that is the same is we are all being looked at. You can only begin to understand another's story if you take the time to read it. Then you can see through the author's perspective. You are writing your story every day. You choose how you take the plot twists. Characters come and go. You choose what those looking at your story read. What you write can be a guide to them as they fill their own pages. Your words change their chapters. Tell your story. I'm so glad I did. I have learned, so now I teach. I have lost; now I love. I have died . . . now I live. I thought my story was over more than once, but new words, new pages, and new characters came long after "the end," with each page better than the last.

I now write a period only because a new sentence is beginning.

You will get through this page; you will grow in this chapter.

Someone bigger than you already knows the story you are writing. Who is holding the pen? Both of you. God gave it to you, but He allows you to give it back. It's like the relationship between an author and an editor.

Trust Him with the pages, the chapters . . . the ending.

Your story continues . . .

and the end is only the beginning.

I know I promised but . . .

I'm just kidding.

The End'ginning . . .

STORY BEHIND THE KEYS

D uring one of my intense hospital stays, my aunt gave me a key necklace with the word "faith" on it. I never took it off, and I always held it tight as a tangible reminder to have faith. At church one night, I was down at the altar praying, and one of the students from the private school I work at came and prayed beside me. As I had my arm around her and was praying over her, God told me to give her my necklace. I had worn it for so long that it was almost a part of me, but I obeyed and put it around her neck. It blessed her so much.

My next key was given to me by my sister-in-law. It said "Fearless," and I wear it all the time. During my toughest battles, I would hold my key, and it was a reminder to be fearless. I have learned that the key to being fearless is trust. If you can build your faith up to the point where no matter how things look, feel, or seem, you trust that God is in control, then all fear is removed. Why do we fear? Usually because it's about something we have no power to control or change, and it's often just a "What if?" This is the perfect time to trust in God's Word and what His promises say and for God to show off His strength—in our weakness. However, we often try to fix things with our own power and try to figure everything out on our own.

Through each season of my battles, new levels of faith have been unlocked. I'm at the place where I have pushed my body to its limits, past the fear of it being too much, because I know that when it's time for that final breath, it will happen when He allows it. It's human nature to reach for a temporary, tangible fix when we get to our weakest point. Prescriptions are filled each day in hope that they will bring some comfort. Depression and anxiety are just a few examples of what happens when we allow our minds to slip into hopelessness and the fearful "What ifs." Then there are the other options the devil offers to "help" with the battles, the weakness, and the suffering. One of those options is drinking; people say they drink to forget. The other option is drugs; they are often used to "space out" and escape current reality. The temporary becomes a lifestyle; the escape becomes a stronghold. There are so many counterfeit options to cope and make it through life's struggles, but the correct one is to simply *trust* Jesus through the suffering and through the fire, knowing His promises to you stand true (see Psalm 34:19). All people go through hard times here on earth, but walking through them with God is the only way. I could not imagine going through what I've been through without God. We have many counterfeit options to help us neglect running to our Heavenly Father, but the amazing news is that He seeks after those who are lost. He is amazing!

I often ask the Lord to teach me the lesson I need to learn during these hard times. I ask Him, "Give me joy through the suffering because I know it won't last forever. Victory is on the other side. As I wait on You, Lord, You renew my strength. This pain will not last, and it's never too late. I trust your timing."

I began to sell these keys to remind people to TRUST God. No matter what the situation is, get your eyes off of it and onto Jesus. Lose all fear, worry, and doubt, and watch new levels of your faith be unlocked.

YOU HAVE THE KEY.

Speaking Before Seeing

I felt I needed to include this topic here at the end of my book, because if there was ever a recipe for healing, speaking life would be a main ingredient. It's beneficial to your body to speak life, but detrimental to speak death. This might seem like a "no-brainer," but I have met so many Bible-believing Christians who speak so negatively when they ask me to pray for their healing. I warn them to watch every word that comes out of their mouths and to look at those words as seeds being planted inside of them. I caution you to do the same. Will you allow your illness to take over or your healing to flourish? The Bible explains that by the stripes of Jesus, "you were healed" (1 Pet. 2:24). That tells me that Cystic Fibrosis is not mine to carry, so I'm leaving it at the foot of the cross, speaking that "I AM HEALED." You should learn to confess this way too. Your words will begin to bring life to your flesh.

We can grow attached to our diagnosis. That is not the way it should be. If you want healing, you have to give up the sickness. In the Bible, Jesus asked the man who sat by the waters each day, "Do you want to be healed?" (John 5:6 ESV). Some people do not want to be without their sickness because they have molded their identity to it, and some even enjoy the attention that comes with it. They can use it as justification for sinning or walking away from God. If you desire healing, speak it before you even see it. This is faith. God asks us to pray specifically, so I have written specific proclamations for Cystic Fibrosis, and I speak these daily. I speak them in the morning and at night, as if they are medication, and I never miss a dosage. I strongly encourage you to do the same. Write your own specific proclamations and speak them over yourself daily. Begin to detach yourself from the illness through your words. This is a vital part of the healing process.

Specific Proclamations to Overcome Cystic Fibrosis

"Lungs be made whole and complete. Every airway is clean and clear, allowing air to flow perfectly without strain. No bacterial growth is allowed, and any scar tissue is removed. My lung function is perfect."

"My pancreas is mucus-free and it releases the exact amount of enzymes and insulin for digestion and absorption. My digestive tract is mucus- and scar-tissue free. My intestines are whole and complete. I gain weight and absorb my nutrition exactly how God intended the human body to do."

"My brain is sharp and clear. I think and remember perfectly. Oxygen flows to my brain as God created it to. Headaches must go in Jesus' name."

"Cystic Fibrosis was cured at the cross. I speak to the mutated DNA gene, and I decree it to be transformed to how God intended it to be. Cystic Fibrosis was plucked up from the root and removed from my body. Every sign and symptom is gone in Jesus' name."

"I declare my immune system is strong and able to fight using the white blood cells my body produces. I command my liver to be clean and without fat. I speak that my heart pumps and blood flows perfectly."

"I walk in perfect health because Jesus paid for my healing. I walk in total healing because Jesus fought and won the battle. I AM MADE WHOLE."

I am a firm believer in speaking specifically to your own body, targeting the exact issue. Also, find some scriptures on healing and speak those out loud too. I began to speak the Word of God about healing, and these specific ones I wrote daily. They became my treatments, along with taking communion daily. Does it really take all of this to gain healing? I don't have that answer nor am I telling you this is the way you must do things. I'm just telling you what I have been doing, and I know it's working for me. His Word will not return void, so you absolutely can't go wrong with speaking it.

Follow My Story

(Actually Follow "His Story" Through Me)